DEATH BY CUBICLE

Recovery From Burnout
Without Quitting Your Job

KELLY L. OWENS

BALBOA.PRESS
A DIVISION OF HAY HOUSE

Copyright © 2022 Kelly L. Owens.

All rights reserved. No part of this book may be used or reproduced by any means, graphic, electronic, or mechanical, including photocopying, recording, taping or by any information storage retrieval system without the written permission of the author except in the case of brief quotations embodied in critical articles and reviews.

Balboa Press books may be ordered through booksellers or by contacting:

Balboa Press
A Division of Hay House
1663 Liberty Drive
Bloomington, IN 47403
www.balboapress.com
844-682-1282

Because of the dynamic nature of the Internet, any web addresses or links contained in this book may have changed since publication and may no longer be valid. The views expressed in this work are solely those of the author and do not necessarily reflect the views of the publisher, and the publisher hereby disclaims any responsibility for them.

The author of this book does not dispense medical advice or prescribe the use of any technique as a form of treatment for physical, emotional, or medical problems without the advice of a physician, either directly or indirectly. The intent of the author is only to offer information of a general nature to help you in your quest for emotional and spiritual well-being. In the event you use any of the information in this book for yourself, which is your constitutional right, the author and the publisher assume no responsibility for your actions.

Any people depicted in stock imagery provided by Getty Images are models, and such images are being used for illustrative purposes only. Certain stock imagery © Getty Images.

Print information available on the last page.

ISBN: 979-8-7652-3179-1 (sc)
ISBN: 979-8-7652-3178-4 (hc)
ISBN: 979-8-7652-3177-7 (e)

Library of Congress Control Number: 2022913690

Balboa Press rev. date: 09/19/2022

For Allen Owens

CONTENTS

Introduction ix

SECTION 1: THE CAUSES AND IMPACT OF BURNOUT

Chapter 1   What Causes Burnout? 1
Chapter 2   The Physical Toll of Burnout from Stress 19
Chapter 3   The Mental, Emotional, and Behavioral Impact of Burnout from Stress 33

SECTION 2: RECOVERY FOR THE BODY

Chapter 4   Get Your Zzzs 43
Chapter 5   Nutrition to Beat Exhaustion 53
Chapter 6   Exercise Away Your Stress 59

SECTION 3: RECOVERY FOR THE MIND

Chapter 7   Change Your Thinking to Change Your Life 67
Chapter 8   Mindfulness Matters 79
Chapter 9   Having an Attitude of Gratitude 85

SECTION 4: RECOVERY FOR THE SPIRIT

Chapter 10   Finding Meaning in Your Work 93
Chapter 11   Seek Joy on a Daily Basis 105
Chapter 12   Feeding Your Spirit 117

Conclusion 121
Endnotes 125
Bibliography 137

INTRODUCTION

That day still stands out in my memory. The thought of writing another report overwhelmed me. I knew what needed to be done, but completing one more repetitive task felt unbearable. Feelings of burnout had been building for some time, but the emotions caught up with me that day. I panicked. With all my coworkers in nearby cubicles, I had to pull it together. I blinked back tears and swallowed the lump in my throat. Running away was not an option. I finally had to address how I was feeling; I could not quit another job. As alone as I might have felt in that moment, my experience was not unique.

Burnout is a growing issue. Despite being identified several decades ago, with a substantial amount of research conducted on the subject, burnout continues to plague many of us. It is having a significant impact within organizations as well. According to a Gallup report, nearly 76% of employees report feeling burned out some of the time, and 28% say they feel that way "very often" or "always" at work. Of the employees reporting feeling burned out, 63% of them are more likely to use sick time and are 2.6 times as likely to be searching for a new job.[1]

> "Recently the World Health Organization included burnout in the latest version of the International Classification of Disease (ICD-11), illustrating the global importance of this 'occupational phenomena.'"[2]

Sometimes we are not in a position to switch jobs. Either the market is not good at the moment, we cannot start over with the limited number of vacation days for new hires, or we cannot risk moving backward in our career track. Moving out of town away from family may prevent job changes as well. Some of us are in the sandwich generation, taking care of the needs of older parents while having children in school.

Sure, we CAN leave one position for another, but we may have valid reasons to stay. Some may accuse us of having limiting beliefs or being trapped by a fear of change. When you have significant factors present outside of work, you think long and hard about your exit strategy. In my case, I was a single mom finally making enough money to pay the mortgage while adding to college savings. I had enough vacation days to take time off from work for events with my daughter, sickness, or other unavoidable reasons. I could visualize possibilities for a better future, but the timing was not right.

Previously when I felt burnout, my pattern had been to quit my job and move to the next one. This time my company promoted me around the time burnout hit, providing a level of pay to help with my daughter's college expenses. There was absolutely no way I could blow this opportunity because I felt burned out! I realized I had to address this pattern of burnout once and for all. I had to stay in this job whether I liked it or not. At the time of publication, I am two years post recovery. Despite having other job offers, I have chosen to remain in this same job. It is possible to recover from burnout without quitting your current job!

There are quite a few books on burnout in used bookstores or one click away on the internet. I skimmed through many, but I could not focus long enough to get any benefit out of them. I needed a quick, easy read that addressed ALL of what was going on with me, not just parts of it.

One day it occurred to me that maybe I was the person to write the book I needed. In this book, I will share what I learned along my journey to recovery from burnout. I hope you come to see me as trusted friend who has been there, done that, and got the medal at the end. I know the dead feeling inside each day as you go through the motions. I know the overwhelming dread and lump in your throat because you want to cry. I know the inside voice screaming for an escape and finding no way out.

The fact is, I was in a three-year cycle of finding work, experiencing burnout, and moving to yet another new job. Not having the option to quit helped me recognize my pattern. A light bulb went off: the burnout kept coming back regardless of the job! I knew others who stayed in their jobs for many years and seemed to be happy. What was different about them?

A key difference for me this time around was that I had grown due to my investment in personal development. I was in the process of developing my own leadership training company as a side gig for college money prior to my promotion. I became certified as a coach to help others increase their self-awareness to overcome obstacles. I previously worked with a nonprofit as an alcohol and drug counselor, and I had obtained a master's degree in management years earlier. I knew the symptoms of burnout, including my lack of passion for my work and feeling like I was not making a difference in the world. I just lacked the full personal awareness of what I could do about it without moving on to a new position.

If you are in a place where you feel burned out in a job not easily cast aside for another, this book was written for you. This book is for those who feel physical and mental exhaustion. It is for those who feel drained in mind, body, and spirit. Although most report burnout in direct relation to work issues, it can also spill over into our personal lives. When you believe you are stuck in a job wasting over forty hours per week, you may begin to question the meaning of it all. There is hope, my friend. You can begin to navigate your way out of burnout while keeping your current job, giving you time to develop an appropriate exit strategy if necessary.

After reflecting on what I found helpful to recover from burnout, I conducted extensive research that validated and supported my suggested tools for recovery. These sources are listed in the notes section and the bibliography. I wanted this book to be more than just my story. It also provides quality information to reference for each unique experience. Not everyone's burnout is exactly the same, but there are common threads. Whatever burnout symptoms you are experiencing, you will find options and resources here for overall wellness.

So, my friend, here is a map of our journey together. First, we will take a moment to gain some understanding of how we get to that place of burnout. We will cover what is going on in our jobs and within us that contributes to it. Next, we will learn about the toll burnout takes on us physically. After that we will move on to understanding what happens mentally and emotionally during burnout.

The next three sections explain how to develop a physical restoration plan, find meaning and joy once again, and learn to manage our thoughts. Remember, I am a repeat burnout offender—four times so far in my life. I have to be diligent about my level of awareness. Creating systems, establishing boundaries, and ensuring time for self-care are all imperative to maintaining recovery.

Each topic was chosen with care to help you get what you need in one concise book. You may be tired and struggling with concentration. You may need to read this book in short segments. Just do what you can as you can. Burnout recovery is a journey, and you do not get from point A to point Z in the blink of an eye. Physical restoration is presented first because addressing physical symptoms may be necessary in order to finish reading the book. You may, however, take each section as it speaks to you. You may be drawn to another section first. That works too. The physical, mental, and spiritual can be addressed in any order that enhances your well-being. The three work together in a synergistic way, so I encourage you to incorporate all three in your recovery. Start with what feels right for you.

The book title was chosen based on something I would say repeatedly to friends and family: I am dying a slow death in my cubicle. In the midst of burnout, I could not see any value in what I was doing. My days dragged on at a painstakingly slow pace. Later, my days became filled with overwhelming stress. It was a place of extremes. Too little challenge and repetitive, routine tasks felt like drudgery. Too much to do and too few resources exaggerated my stress level. Those extremes fuel burnout, and as we are burning out, we feel we are dying a slow death. It is possible to take control of your thoughts and feelings to manage these extremes until the conditions on the job change. You can download a free companion workbook at www.revealedpotential.com.

SECTION 1

The Causes And Impact Of Burnout

CHAPTER 1

What Causes Burnout?

Remember my three-year pattern? For a long time, I thought I had bad luck getting jobs that sucked the life out of me. It can be tempting to quit a job you believe leaves you feeling exhausted with no enthusiasm for life. However, if I had continued to change jobs every three years, I would not have learned what I am going to share with you in this book. What I did not know then that I know now is there are things I can do to help prevent me from getting into that dark place again. In this chapter, you will learn what burnout is, situational factors that contribute to it, and who is more prone to developing burnout.

Researchers have spent years digging into the various aspects of burnout. In the 1970s, the term burnout mainly began to be used to describe what workers in the human services field frequently experienced.[3] To date, there are forty-five years' worth of research out there on burnout.

Rather than overwhelming you with all the research, I will share what I found helpful in my recovery. Some areas may be a bit technical, but I hope you will find beneficial details to aid in your own recovery.

Early research on burnout focused on those working in the human services field and was more about the relationship between the service provider and client.[4] A great deal of the older research focused on burnout in physicians, nurses, medical school students, interns, counselors, teachers, and the clergy. It was geared toward those in direct services with an emotional component in the provider-client relationship. However, burnout can occur in any profession. I personally experienced burnout while working as an addictions counselor, in human resources work, in nonprofit leadership, and in the business sector in the automotive industry. Later studies began to look at those in occupations related to business. The focus shifted to the relationship to one's work, allowing for an expanded understanding of the phenomena in other professions.[5]

Christina Maslach is well known for her studies on burnout. The Maslach Burnout Inventory was originally developed to measure the symptoms of burnout in those who worked in human service occupations, and it has frequently been used as an assessment tool to identify burnout in study participants. Over time, other versions have been developed for use with medical personnel, teachers, those in human services, and general use for occupations other than human services and education.[6] As new findings were discovered in burnout research, the need for assessment tools in a variety of occupations became apparent. If you are curious if you officially qualify as burned out, you can use a free version of a burnout survey to find out. The website is listed in the notes for chapter one.[7]

If you believe you are burned out, you probably are. As you read through the book and recognize symptoms that apply to you, I encourage you to look at those areas and implement the suggestions to address your areas of concern.

Most of the research states that burnout has three dimensions to it: emotional exhaustion, depersonalization, and inefficacy.[8]

Exhaustion is the most commonly reported symptom of burnout. It comes about from experiencing too many job demands for an extended period of time. Exhaustion comes from being overworked and under resourced. The daily stress builds to a point when we eventually feel worn out. The various demands of my past jobs, lack of emotional support, and scarcity of resources to carry out my duties led to emotional exhaustion, which turned into physical exhaustion. Eventually getting out of bed in the morning was very difficult. There were days when I felt I might collapse at work. When we are feeling exhausted, it is difficult to face challenges without having some emotional overreaction. I outwardly avoided meltdowns at work, but on the inside, I was a mess. At times I had to pull myself together in a bathroom stall.

Depersonalization is also known as cynicism. This is when we emotionally distance ourselves from the stress of the job demands. Reflecting back, my depersonalization behaviors were an attempt to ignore how overwhelmed I felt. I experienced less empathy for my clients' issues when working in social service. This was also true for how I viewed the demands of customers in the business sector. Early on, I would be an enthusiastic helper, wanting to solve every problem that came down the pike. Eventually as I became overwhelmed and exhaustion set in, I did not have the resources to deal with their never-ending issues with the same energy I once had. Most demands were met with annoyance. The cynicism was exposed by statements like "nothing will ever change around here" or "I am so sick of . . ." That blank could be filled in by numerous options!

Inefficacy is the belief that what we are doing has no meaning. We question if we are effective in our roles anymore, and this feeling can extend to questioning if life is being wasted staying in this occupation. I questioned how effective I was at managing my workload and making any kind of difference. I not only felt ineffective in my day-to-day work but questioned if there was any meaning for me to continue what I was doing. Reaching this point typically prompted me to find a new job. Overall, I had times of feeling like an utter failure. I was frustrated, feeling trapped in a job that left me unhappy and unfulfilled. We have to find meaning in our work to feel some level of personal fulfillment. Otherwise, it feels like we are simply doing time. We ask, "Is this as good as it gets?" My measures of success were defined by the potential for advancement, appropriate compensation, and providing meaningful contributions. These criteria were not being met most days.

Internal and external factors contribute to our burnout. As I just mentioned, I often felt frustrated that I was in yet another situation that wore me out and left me feeling like a failure. Not all of that unhappiness can be blamed on the job, however. Certainly there are factors in the job environment that stoke burnout, but the truth is we personally add to it as well. That is good news, though, because it means we have control over how we contribute to burnout personally and can prevent it going forward.

External Factors That Contribute to Burnout

Job Characteristics

All jobs come with demands, and we need resources to help support us in meeting those demands. However, when the demands exceed the resources provided, we find ourselves paying a mental, emotional, and physical price. Many studies have examined the relationship between burnout, job demands, and job resources.

A detailed study on burnout and engagement tested several hypotheses related to job demands, jobs resources, burnout, engagement, health issues, and intention to quit. They found:

1. Burnout is an intermediary between job demands and health issues.

2. Engagement is an intermediary between job resources and intention to leave the job.[9]

Increasing job demands were found to be positively related to the presence of burnout and health issues, while access to adequate job resources was found to be positively related to being engaged on the job and a reduced likelihood of intentions to quit. These results indicate relationships between the variables tested but do not necessarily imply causality.

Engagement was seen as the opposite of burnout and is defined as being "a positive, fulfilling, work-related state of mind."[10] We will cover more on this later when we examine what can be done to address the issues related to depersonalization and the feelings of inefficacy. Those who experience engagement are feeling a sense of energy, dedication, and meaning in their work. In burnout, we experience exhaustion, detachment through cynicism, and loss of meaning.

What exactly are the job demands that lead to burnout? They can be the physical conditions on the job, workload, time constraints, and client or management demands. Job resources are intended to reduce the demands, but a lack of resources along with high demands creates the perfect storm for burnout. According to one study, "Job resources refer to those physical, psychological, social, or organizational aspects of the job that may do any of the following: (a) be functional in achieving work goals; (b) reduce job demands at the associated physiological and psychological costs; (c)stimulate personal growth and development."[11]

As I discuss my experiences below, what I share is not a criticism of any organization where I have been involved. I believe many work issues occur due to ignorance, lack of other resources to support higher-level leadership, and people doing the best they can with what resources they have. I look back at my past jobs with an open heart and gratitude for what I learned. I am grateful for having known the people I met at each place.

When I worked at a treatment center as a fairly new addictions counselor, I did not get the support and feedback I needed. I managed an ever-growing case load. Many of my experienced coworkers were in recovery from addiction and working professionally as counselors. Sadly, I found that many of my fellow counselors, who I needed as mentors, were not in a healthy place to mentor me. Professionally I could determine many were in relapse and not managing it. Over time, I was not sure what advice to trust. It left me feeling frustrated and alone. I would attend professional development trainings, hear about best practices, and quickly see the gaps we had with best practices in our organization. One of my values was to provide quality services to clients. I worried that we were falling short due to the issues I saw present in the treatment center.

In another setting working as the director of a local nonprofit, I had very little support from the original Board of Directors. In fact, when I walked into this organization, I found that many of the board members were not committed at the level needed for this small nonprofit to thrive. Our mission was to build affordable housing for those in need. I felt pressured to find the funding to build a house all on my own. The board did not help with fundraising or strategic planning, and operations had been in a dormant state for two years prior to my arrival. What funds they had barely kept the place afloat. There were not enough resources to build another house and serve another family! Organizations cannot recover overnight from that kind of neglect. It took another eighteen months to begin to see the fruits of a lot of labor to start a house build. By that time, board members had changed, and the new ones were significantly more supportive. Eventually several more houses were built, and more families were served. However, I had grown very tired by that point. The organization was finally thriving, but I did not know how to replenish my own resources.

Both of these examples in nonprofits included direct aspects of social services. I was impacted by my relationship to the work and serving people. As any doctor, nurse, social worker, police office, first responder, pastor, or counselor can tell you, the needs of other people can be draining. It can also be very frustrating when you feel like you are working harder to reach the goal than the client you are serving. Often cynicism becomes a coping mechanism to put emotional distance between you and needy clients.

After a while, I began to wonder if the treatment center clients were only in treatment to comply with probation. In the nonprofit housing program, I began to believe the people we served were not grateful for all that had been done for them. I cynically believed they would blow off mortgage payments again to buy the next expensive cell phone. I did not want to hear any more sob stories because they could not manage their money. After I wore myself out trying to find funds to get an affordable house built, I did not want to hear any excuses. I wanted them to hold up their end of the agreement. This carried over into being cynical about new applicants to the program too. I started to believe everyone was running a con game. I questioned my ability to make an impact in people's lives when the opportunities others worked so hard to provide were wasted. But not all applicants were running a con game, and not all the homeowners were ungrateful or entitled. My perception of things was a result of burnout.

In the for-profit sector, trying to meet key performance indicators can be just as draining when the targets are unattainable or in conflict with other team's targets. For example, in my supply chain position, I saw competing demands that lacked adequate resources. When different segments of the supply chain had different timelines that did not match up with each other, problems arose. The lack of collaboration along the nodes of the supply chain allowed this problem to continue. Not only can there be mismatches between teams that add to stress, but also mismatches between us and other areas of our jobs.

Some of the mismatches found by researchers are:[12]

- Workload
- Control
- Reward
- Community
- Fairness
- Values

As you can see, many of these align with the job demands and resources. When our workloads are too much for one person to effectively manage, we can get burned out. A workload mismatch may also be the wrong kind of work if we lack the skills or desire for that kind of work.[13]

Having no control over how we manage our day and tasks can also lead to problems. A worker's control over time and decision making is a job resource.[14] One frustrating experience my coworkers and I regularly had was a past supervisor allowing other teams to dump their work on us, even though this work included illogical tasks for the prescribed roles and responsibilities of our team. He would never establish boundaries, and we often had more work to do with little notice to complete it. It was hard to produce quality outcomes in those cases. It is a mismatch when responsibility for outcomes exceeds the capacity to deliver as well.[15] Additionally, having extra duties that were not appropriate for our team created frustration, confusion, and resentment. After a while, it was hard to know what was expected of us because we were not clear on our roles. Role clarity helps alleviate burnout as another job resource.[16]

A reward mismatch may be financial, but it can also occur when efforts are not acknowledged.[17] Recognition adds value to the work and the worker. This lack of reward is related to feelings of inefficacy. Recently I wrote about how a lack of feedback reduces workplace engagement. In the book *Voices of Leadership-Volume 1*, my chapter focuses on being the kind of leader whose feedback is well received. People like to know how they are doing and if what they are doing is making a difference.

Regarding the mismatch of community, a sense of positive social connection enhances a worker's experience. If the work leads to being isolated or social contact is impersonal, employees do not get the benefit of social support as a resource, especially if conflict is present.[18] We are seeing more of this due to working from home, which increased across fields during the pandemic. Enjoying the social aspects of work and support systems with like-minded coworkers helps us feel a sense of community. One study found that coworker support leads to reduced perceptions of burnout.[19]

Lack of fairness is seen as a serious mismatch and is demonstrated through inequity of pay, promotions, handling grievances, being given a voice, and evaluations. It often fuels the cynicism seen in burnout.[20] I have observed a supervisor regularly make excuses for one team member despite repeated poor performance. Another team member, being a very conscientious worker who cared about the team's performance, took on more and more duties to cover for the coworker's ineptitude. Eventually resentment grew, and the one carrying an extra heavy load grew exhausted and cynical. The higher the perceived levels of distributive justice, the lower the perceived burnout levels among employees.[21]

Values are of great significance. We cannot continue to engage in activities that go against our values. If you are working in a place with unethical practices, I do encourage you to begin developing your exit strategy as soon as you can. However, in some cases values may be where the organizational goals do not align with our personal career aspirations, a gap exists between the lofty mission statement and actual practices, or values conflict between departments, such as cost containment and excellent customer service.[22]

Work to Family Conflict

Work to family conflict occurs when the job begins to interfere with family life. Earlier I mentioned that in one nonprofit job I began to have work and family conflicts. Sometimes my weekend hours resulted in missing time with my daughter. Additionally, there were some evening obligations that interfered with being home to help her with homework and prepare dinner. At the time I was still married to her father, so we could work out a schedule, but that did not alleviate the stress for me.

This mismatch can occur in any field. In an article about finding balance between work and everything else, the author, a physician, cited work to family conflict as the top common factor contributing to burnout among gastroenterologists. Survey results indicated that 52% of the surgeons had a work to home conflict in the prior three weeks and of that number, 37% had a higher rate of burnout.[23] Missing important family events due to work conflicts heightens our stress, and missing out on what we value leads to a diminished sense of well-being in life.

It has been found that the work to family conflict can be a powerful predictor of burnout.[24] I believe this ties in well with our values. We want to protect what we value, and we feel stress if we do not believe we are doing a good job of protecting it.

Does Age, Gender, or Marital Status Play a Role?

Research seems to indicate that the variances in predicting burnout by gender are dependent on the type of occupation.[25] The symptoms of burnout can show up differently for men and woman. Women report more exhaustion than men across a variety of occupations and were more likely to have work to family conflicts.[26] This may be due to women carrying many of the traditional expectations when it comes to taking care of children and the household along with having to work outside the home. Men were found to have more frequent reports of depersonalization or cynicism.[27] This, too, may be due to how men have been socialized. It may be related to the messages encouraging men to be tough, not display emotion, and carry the burdens in life on their shoulders.

Despite what the research indicates, there can be variations. Each one of us is different, and we come from diverse backgrounds. As a female, I have experienced cynicism. The emotional exhaustion always hits me first, though. As someone who becomes emotionally invested in my work, I want to have purpose and make a difference. When I feel drained due to endless demands and lack of resources, I move into a protective stance with depersonalization or cynicism.

Even though a lower burnout score for married employees was found compared to non-married, the difference was small.[28] Marital status in and of itself is not reliable as a possible predictor for who will experience burnout. Neither can parental status. Those having children actually scored lower than those who were childless.[29] The earlier mention of work to family conflicts would seem to be confounding. I believe the key variable here has more to do with the actual occupation than simply having a family or not having a family.

When I reviewed studies looking at age, it appeared that occupation also played a role. Some studies showed younger employees were more likely to experience burnout, while others showed it was more likely in older employees in the occupation being studied. I know from personal experience I had burnout in my twenties with no children and again in my late forties as a mother.

In having the benefit of looking back on past experiences, I would say my burnout was due to the same kinds of job and personal factors across the years. For me, my gender, age, and marital status were not determining factors.

Internal Factors

The Big Five Personality Traits

Now that we have looked at some external factors, we need to move on some of the internal factors that lead to burnout. As part of my recovery, I had to take ownership of the areas where I was contributing to my burnout. Once I gained the awareness that I was a repeat burnout offender, I had to identify my thoughts and behaviors that fueled burnout. I also had to accept the fact that I was the one responsible for making the necessary changes. No one could do this for me.

In developing a deeper understanding of burnout, researchers began to look at personality types. The Big Five personality traits are referenced in many studies. The five traits are extraversion, agreeableness, conscientiousness, neuroticism, and autonomy.[30]

Extraverted people tend to be more social and confident. They seek interactions with others. This characteristic is shown to have a negative relationship with burnout.[31] This makes sense because connection is shown to reduce burnout. Extraverts find support when interacting with others.

Agreeableness is about being open-minded and willing to hear new information. People with this personality trait do not feel threatened by new situations or people. Conscientious people are apt to solve problems in challenging situations rather than embracing a sense of hopelessness. In studying positive psychology, I have learned that this trait leads to resilience, a hallmark of well-being.

Neuroticism leads to not handling stress well. People with this trait tends to have strong emotional reactions to stressful situations.[32] Some people grow up with parents who model these traits. I regularly saw my mother become extremely anxious when problems arose. Fear of the worst-case scenario led to her anxiety. Alternatively, my dad would not immediately assume the worst and would calmly suggest solutions. What we think leads to how we feel and how we act. When we are prone to strong emotional reactions, we can contribute to our own burnout. Neuroticism was found to be positively related to emotional exhaustion, depersonalization, and inefficacy.[33]

In stressful situations, those with neuroticism tend to have wishful thinking, self-blame, distancing from others, and anxiety.[34] This is in direct opposition of resilience and well-being. It lacks a realistic view of situations and tends to magnify problems. We will cover more about distortions of thinking to address this as part of recovery.

Extraversion and agreeableness were positively correlated with personal accomplishment.[35] They help prevent the feelings of inefficacy seen with burnout. A more open-minded and gentle view of one's efforts replaces harsh criticism. Connection with others helps us gain other points of view rather than getting lost in our own thoughts, which can be distorted.

Lack of Self-Care

It is easy to fall into the trap of not taking care of oneself. We like to believe that we have it together and we are fine. By avoiding self-care, we put off paying real attention to the warning signs caused by stress and our emotions.

One of my personal warning signs, which I am now very aware of, is the tension in my shoulder blades and base of my neck. I would only notice it once the pain really set in, and I could not find relief from it. My muscles were telling me all along that my level of stress was rising, and I was not noticing, like the fable about the frog in a pot of boiling water. It suggests cooking the frog by putting it in cold water over a low flame. Little by little the water heats up, but the frog does not notice. Eventually the water boils, and it is too late for that poor frog.

As mentioned above, people with neuroticism do not manage stress well. Those with this trait have higher scores for sedation, withdrawal, wishful thinking, self-blame, and escapist fantasy as methods for coping.[13] None of those reactions are self-care. Sedation is anything we do to numb ourselves to what we are feeling. Withdrawal can include things like zoning out into television or not sharing feelings with a trusted loved one. We may avoid joining fun events because we just want to be alone.

To be completely transparent, I would be categorized as neurotic. That word seems like a label for having a mental health issue. Sadly, mental health issues still carry a stigma in our society. You may be feeling some resistance right now to what is being presented. The reality is that mental health is a continuum from healthy to unhealthy. I am simply not at the side of completely healthy, but I am certainly not at the other end of completely unhealthy either. Fortunately, mental health is fluid, and we can change! Please do not believe the lie that your personality can never be changed. Mine has been evolving over the years, and it is now more positive and healthier than it was in my much younger years.

Sedation for me also surfaces by eating junk food. For others it might be alcohol or drugs. I am a stress eater and get into a vicious cycle of sweet and salty cravings when I feed that craving monster. Weight gain is my big, flashing neon sign that I am not managing stress. I have a tendency toward withdrawal because I just want everyone to leave me alone. When I am in that place, I do not want to crack the door open to anyone who might want something from me that I just do not have to give. I fear anyone will drain me of what reserves I have left.

When I tell myself that my stress is temporary, no real solutions are considered. Wishful thinking sugarcoats reality. Often, I will push myself harder, believing I need to do better. I harshly critique myself and give myself a low score for not having tried hard enough. I make myself depressed with fantasy, imagining that life would be better if this happened or that happened, or I entertain thoughts of running away to a life I would prefer.

When we fall into patterns of wishful thinking, we can get caught in vicious cycles that not only contribute to burnout but also exacerbate it. Lack of good sleep, not stepping away to destress, not reducing demands on our calendars, not cutting ourselves some slack, eating a poor diet, and not exercising all lead to health issues. We will take a deeper look at this shortly, but if you are experiencing these symptoms, I want you to know that you are not alone. There are solutions to help you change things for the better.

Not Reaching Out for Help

Reaching out for help when you need it can be a struggle. If you are like me, you may be stuck in the mindset that you do not want to burden anyone. I grew up believing that I should never be a burden to anyone, and I have been reluctant to reach out for help when I needed it. As I have grown in my self-development, however, I have come to see the value in having connections and support. It is amazing how reaching out for suggestions from others can help. It truly helps reduce stress to honestly share your struggles with someone. Simply unloading all that inner turmoil and confusion can help lighten the load.

Where Do We Go from Here?

This has been a detailed chapter about burnout, how it happens, and how it shows up. With this foundation, you can see why simply quitting your job will not solve the problem. Developing your exit strategy requires you to increase your awareness of what causes burnout. You do not want to jump into another job and simply repeat the old pattern. You will need to discern what you want to be different moving forward. As we look at how to recover in the following chapters, you will have the tools to break the cycle when you decide it is time to find your next job. This is a journey, my friend, and I am right here with you each step of the way.

CHAPTER 2

The Physical Toll of Burnout from Stress

Who Is That Person in the Mirror?

If you are suffering from burnout, you may not like what you see in the mirror some mornings. During my own periods of burnout, I had dark circles under my eyes that required more makeup concealer. The more I used, however, the more it settled into my wrinkles. This was certainly not the look I hoped to achieve!

Overall, I did not have that healthy glow about me. I have met people older than myself who still radiated health and younger people who simply looked worn out. I personally attribute all this difference to chronic unmanaged stress. I have also been guilty of this. Even now, with all that I have learned, I have to be very intentional about managing my stress.

This chapter addresses the physical toll chronic stress can have on us. Managing your stress is incredibly important to your overall well-being. It is too easy to get into an avoidance mindset. Remember in the frog story how the temperature slowly rises, but the frog does not realize it? Chronic stress gradually creates health problems that build and compound as time goes on.

Stress affects the major systems of the body, and unmanaged stress results in unwanted health outcomes. If we are unaware something is a problem, we definitely will not take action to address it. To get to the other side of your burnout recovery journey, you have to take care of your body as well as your mind. There are things you want to do in the future, and your body will need to be able to serve you to accomplish those things.

Systems Affected by Chronic Stress

Our endocrine, cardiovascular, gastrointestinal, respiratory, and musculoskeletal systems are impacted by chronic stress.[36] You may notice certain negative changes in your body when you feel chronic stress. When I do not manage it well, I have terrible food cravings that lead to weight gain. I do not sleep as well and have achy muscles in my neck and shoulders. Others may experience digestive issues, elevated blood pressure, hair loss, and a variety of other symptoms.

In a webinar I attended, a man shared about his burnout and the stress he was under all the time. I could relate to a lot of what he talked about because I had a similar experience with corporate culture. Our parent companies were in the same country, so the structure and management style were very much the same. As a successful, high-ranking executive, he discussed the lack of local control resulting from an overseas parent company. He experienced growing demands and a never-ending focus on failures by management. Management never noticed when things went right, but they would grill him over the one thing that did not go well. Eventually the stress began to affect his thinking, and then it began to show up physically. He kept pushing himself until he felt like he was on the verge of a nervous breakdown. He felt ill one evening and had to excuse himself from attending a business dinner. As the night wore on, he lost his ability to verbalize his thoughts and became partially paralyzed on one side. He was placed on short-term disability and was away from work for around four months. Despite all his successes for that company, he knew being away for that time would cost him his career with them. It took him another year to regain his health. He learned a lot from this experience and now knows the value of stress management.

No job is worth your health, even if you are unable to resign from it. You have to realize that only you can take care of yourself. Good leaders recognize the limits of their people and work with them to reduce demands and offer more resources. Many of us work for people who have managerial titles but lack the awareness of a strong leader. These managers simply miss the clues their team members give when they are reaching their limits. You cannot wait around for someone to give you permission to take care of yourself.

The Endocrine System

Our bodies were designed to deal with dangers in our environment through the release of hormones, commonly known as the fight or flight response. In the past, the dangers humans faced were more life-or-death than what modern humans generally face. Of course, there are still life-or-death dangers all over the world, but the stress response we have to job pressures and other social situations is often the same as if we were in life-or-death situations.

To respond to stress, the body releases hormones. There are two categories of hormones—catecholamines (epinephrine/adrenalin and norepinephrine/noradrenaline) and glucocorticoids (cortisol and corticosterone) that coordinate the body's response to stress.[37] When the amygdala in the brain detects a stressor, it regulates emotions such as fear and aggression.[38] It is similar to a house alarm. When a door opens, the warning beeps sound, giving about thirty seconds to enter a code to shut off the alarm. This is similar to how your amygdala determines if a threat exists or not. If the code is not entered quickly enough, the full alarm goes off. At this point, the amygdala signals the brain stem to release catecholamines.[39] This is like your alarm system company contacting you to see if you need help. Adrenalin and noradrenalin are the catecholamines known for the flight or fight response. Their goal is to have an effect on systems that get you ready to run from dangers or stay and fight them. This is the acute stress response. One of the most commonly known physical responses is an increased heart rate. The release of adrenalin and noradrenalin leads to increasing heart rate, shutting down digestion, using stored glucose for energy, and readying the muscles and nervous system for fight or flight.[40]

The amygdala also sends a signal to the hypothalamus to release corticotropin releasing hormone (CRH).[41] Just like the alarm system, if you do not respond to their call to check if you need help, they automatically contact the police. The glucocorticoids are slower to exert their effect on the body and can be detected about 20-30 minutes after the onset of a stressor.[42] This begins a process known as the Hypothalamic-Pituitary-Adrenal Axis, or the HPA Axis. Next the pituitary gland responds to the presence of CRH by releasing ACTH (adreno-corticotropic hormone), which then signals the release of cortisol by the adrenal gland.[43]

In a normally functioning system, once cortisol is released, it signals back to the brain to shut off the release of any more cortisol as a means to protect the body from prolonged exposure, which is detrimental.[44] If the HPA system is frequently activated, it can lead to a malfunction resulting in excess cortisol. Excess cortisol can be detected in saliva testing. Having excess cortisol can lead to detrimental health outcomes including hypertension and impaired immune function.[45]

The Link Between Chronic Stress and Overeating

There is a relationship between chronic stress and overeating. An excess intake of calories can lead to obesity. In particular, "excess cortisol concentrations have been associated with visceral fat accumulation."[46] Visceral fat is the accumulation of fat in the abdominal cavity, and it can build up in our arteries. We have to have enough energy to deal with daily life demands. Our energy comes from food, however, we can feel the urge to eat more than required under chronic stress conditions.

A complex feedback loop occurs before the brain stops releasing cortisol, similar to the fight or flight response. Hormones also help us to know when we are hungry or full. One study suggested a regulatory feedback loop between CRH and another hormone called Neuropeptide Y (NPY).[47] When excess CRH is released, it can stimulate appetite. In the feedback loop mentioned, NPY plays a role in food intake. In a healthy system, they regulate each other because CRH inhibits the release of NPY. If there is excess CRH, which stimulates appetite, it is not regulating NPY. Insulin and leptin also play a role in satiety. Increases in glucocorticoids have been associated with leptin and insulin resistance.[48] This resistance can lead to our inability to pick up on the signals that we are full.

Studies show a relationship between stress eating and reward centers in our brain, which helps to explain the concept of comfort foods. "Increased glucocorticoid secretion following HPA axis activation appears to be a central pathway through which stress promotes the consumption of palatable food."[49] When we eat something that brings us pleasure, thus momentarily removing the negative stress, we reinforce the behavior to reach for comfort foods to get relief. I know I crave junk food and fatty comfort foods when I am in a state of chronic stress, meaning I recognize those cravings a potential warning sign.

Highly palatable foods can activate the same reward system of the brain as drugs of abuse.[50] As a former addictions counselor, I have seen how easily we can reinforce behaviors that seek pleasure to avoid pain. Combined with the biochemical factors of unregulated hormones and resistance, it is no wonder we stress eat.

When I manage my stress and eat healthy foods, those cravings subside to levels where I can more easily say no to temptations. I am able to get back on the path to healthy eating without being controlled by my cravings.

Adrenal Fatigue

Adrenal fatigue is not an accepted medical diagnosis according to Mayo Clinic and Harvard Health Publishing at Harvard Medical School. The adrenal glands produce hormones, as mentioned earlier in looking at how cortisol is released. There can be adrenal *insufficiencies*, and those can be diagnosed by your doctor through blood tests. Your fatigue can be caused by many factors, including stress, poor sleep, poor diet, and underlying medical conditions. Excessive stress can make us tired; however, "adrenal fatigue" is not supported by empirical research or by the medical community. Please be wary of products available online that promise to address adrenal fatigue. Talk to your doctor for help in determining if any other issues are present in addition to the effects of stress.

The Cardiovascular System

As mentioned in the section about the endocrine system, catecholamines are released in response to stress. Prolonged exposure to stress hormones can cause damaging effects to the heart and brain, leading to heart attack and stroke due to:

- Increased oxygen demands on the body
- Spasms of the coronary blood vessels
- Electrical instability in the heart's conduction system
- Increased blood pressure
- Abnormal heart rhythms [51]

Think back to the story I shared about the man who lost his ability to speak and was paralyzed on one side of his body. His stress levels remained too high for too long, resulting in severe physical impairment.

Job strain can lead directly to chronic stress, which also has a relationship with coronary heart disease. It makes sense that high job strain can be a contributing factor to coronary heart disease. High job strain is also associated with increased serum cholesterol and increases in body mass index (BMI).[52] Excess cortisol leads to visceral fat, which along with stress eating can cause weight gain. My physician has told me to reduce my sugar and fat intake, as both have an impact on my cholesterol levels.

Cortisol normally reduces inflammation, but the excess secretion of it can actually lead to resistance of its anti-inflammatory properties and vulnerability to atherosclerosis.[53] Atherosclerosis is also known as hardening of the arteries due to plaque buildup. A feedback loop usually signals the release of cortisol to stop, but chronic stress may cause a dysregulation of that system. I was shocked when plaque showed up in my eyes during an eye exam. This led to a carotid artery ultrasound to be sure I was not in danger of a stroke. I was only 41 years old at the time!

> Increased levels of the inflammatory markers C-reactive protein and interleukin-6 have been found to predict a coronary event. Work stress is linked to increased levels of epinephrine

(adrenaline) which might have a role in upregulating inflammatory cytokines, along with activating platelets (blood clotting) and macrophages (a white blood cell that is part of immune system). Along with cortisol, it can also lead to glucose intolerance, high blood pressure and high cholesterol—all part of what is called metabolic syndrome.[54]

As I read the research to write this section of the book, it truly drove home the point that I must keep stress management in the forefront. I have cholesterol issues and struggle to maintain a healthy BMI if not careful with my diet. Some of this is hereditary, but by not addressing stress, I only compound the existing problems. Stress exacerbates hereditary issues, and in order to have the quality of life that I want, I have to be proactive about my stress management and overall health.

During times of very high stress, I have experienced severe chest pains. It happened quite a few times during the end of my prior marriage while in a job that was already leading to burnout. My stress was at an all-time high. Sharp pains shot through my back, between my shoulder blades, and in my chest. It happened again a few years later while trying to organize a conference. I had a lot of demands and few resources for that project at the time. I remember debating whether I should get medical help or not. Of course, true to form, I disregarded my stress because I was too busy and had deadlines. Fortunately, no evidence of a heart attack has been found, but stress-related chest pains are a significant reminder that chronic stress has gone unmanaged for way too long.

The Gastrointestinal System

Chronic stress can affect our gastrointestinal system as well. One study measured the intestinal contractions of rats in a stress induced state. The results lead to increased motility, or the increased movement of waste through the bowels, along with volume.[55] During times of high stress, it is quite common to have stomach upset or need to make emergency trips to the bathroom.

People who already have irritable bowel syndrome (IBS) find their symptoms worsened by stress, just as those who have dyspepsia (indigestion or discomfort in upper abdomen) also find stress leads to the feeling of indigestion.[56] If you already suffer from these conditions, it is imperative you begin to take stress management seriously.

In recent years we have heard a lot about gut health and pre- and pro-biotics. It has been discovered that there is a gut-brain axis, which is a two-way connection that benefits both the digestive system and the brain.[57] What happens in our gut can impact our brains. When I began to take a pre- and pro-biotic as a way to address my exhaustion, I felt better. My stomach was upset less of the time, and the longer I took them, the more energy I had. A study released in September 2021 found that neurodegenerative systems were reduced by the anti-oxidative properties of pre- and pro-biotics.[58]

Oxidative stress can lead to the neurodegenerative diseases such Alzheimer's and Parkinson's. Eating a plant-based diet, adding pre- and pro-biotics as supplements, and making sure our guts are healthy could possibly reduce the likelihood and impact of these conditions.

There are multiple mechanisms underlying oxidative stress. Concentrations of the reactive oxygen species (ROS) need to remain in balance because over or underproduction causes cellular damage.[59] Commercials for antioxidant supplements often mention these free radicals.

Maintaining our gastrointestinal health matters not only for how our stomachs feel but also because of its impact on our brains. The next chapter will dive deeper into this relationship.

The Musculoskeletal System

Those with stress-induced cortisol dysfunction show signs of bone and muscle breakdown, fatigue, and pain.[60] When stressed, we walk around tensing muscles and may not even realize it. I feel achy in my shoulders, upper back, neck, and lower back. When I have a massage, a good part of the hour is spent just working on the knots in my upper back.

Steven Chaney, PhD, described which muscles are affected by stress in his August 2020 blog. He pointed out the top three affected are:

- **Levator Scapulae** (shrug muscles) — These get shortened over time due to tensing up and then pull on the cervical vertebrae. He believes this leads to headaches.
- **Intercostals** (muscles between rib bones) — Under stress we may breathe shallowly or hold our breath, causing these muscles to shorten. When we breathe deeply, they stretch.
- **Masseter** (jaw and hinge, where back teeth are located) — Under stress we sometimes clench our jaws and shorten this muscle over time. This can lead to temporomandibular joint dysfunction (TMJ), where your jawbone "clicks" over the bone above your ear. It can be painful.[61]

Not only do we feel achy, but there can be more going on with our musculoskeletal system due to chronic stress. As discussed in the prior sections, unmanaged stress can lead to inflammation due to the excess cortisol. Inflammation also leads to oxidative stress. Oxidative stress occurs when there is an imbalance between free radicals in your body and antioxidants. It is not a disease, but rather a by-product of normal cellular function. "In humans, stress-induced inflammation has been implicated in diseases such as osteoporosis, rheumatoid arthritis, myopathy, fibromyalgia, chronic fatigue syndrome, chronic pelvic pain, temporomandibular joint dysfunction, chronic low back pain, sciatica and more."[62]

It can be easy to start taking over-the-counter pain relievers more frequently to get relief from these aches and pains, but these don't address the underlying issue. Instead, we need to implement stress management techniques and exercise to get relief from tight muscles naturally.

The Respiratory System

As mentioned above, stress often leads to shallow breathing or moments of holding our breath. When we are relaxed, we inhale oxygen deeply and fully exhale. Emotions and stress play a role in many diseases, and respiratory illnesses are no exception.[63]

Acute stress is short term, and our bodies can adapt to meet the required needs with the fight or flight response. When the stressor is eliminated, we return to normal levels to allow for recovery. This allows for tissue to regenerate and chemical levels to return back into balance. With prolonged stress, our body stays in a state of excess demand. This is when we see the damage caused by the dysregulation of HPA axis and the resulting oxidative stress.

One major effect of repeated stress is the exacerbation of the chronic inflammatory response, which can lead to increased long-term damage of the airway.[64] If you already have certain pulmonary disorders, long-term stress could magnify those issues. In particular, asthma is a disease worsened by chronic stress.[65] Stress affects every major system in the body, and I hope you are beginning to see the value in stress management. Until I really dug into the research, it never occurred to me that unmanaged stress could affect my body to this degree. I knew I needed to feel calmer, and that stress generally was not healthy, but I really was ignorant of the severity of the damage it could cause.

The Immune System

When we disregard self-care and stress management, we choose to compromise our immune health. Our immune system helps us fight off illness. Chronic stress impacts our immune system just as it does our endocrine, cardiovascular, gastrointestinal, muscular, and respiratory systems.

One study reviewed the impact of chronic stress and the specific effects on the immune system. Most chronic stressors are associated with decreases in almost all functional immune measures.[66] We have a variety of cells and chemicals in our body to help fight off infection, protect other cells, and prevent inflammation. Their ability to perform those functions is decreased when we live in a state of chronic stress.

White blood cells are a key defense against foreign invaders. Larger white cells, called phagocytes, swallow foreign particles.[67] The other white blood cells, lymphocytes, help our body to remember prior invaders and fight off infection or disease. There are two types of lymphocytes: B cells for releasing antibodies and T cells that attack target cells infected by viruses.[68] Chronic stress decreases our white blood cell counts, leaving us more vulnerable to illness.

There are also special chemical communicators within the immune system called cytokines.[69] These are produced by a variety of cells including the B cells and T cells. They help to regulate immunity. One interesting study looked at the relationship between chronic stress and the presence of cytokines in the saliva of the participants. These chemicals are either pro-inflammatory or anti-inflammatory. The study was conducted with Mexican immigrants identified with chronic stress due to fear of deportation. Pro-inflammatory cytokines were found in participant saliva samples, and this was linked to the chronic stress levels the participants experienced.[70]

Chronic stress creates issues in our immune system that can lead to additional health issues. In order to keep the immune system strong, we have to reduce stress, eat healthy, get exercise, and get enough sleep.

Skin and Hair

Chronic stress also impacts our hair and skin. There is a new area of specialty that researches the connection between our skin and our brain. The skin has been found to be a key target for stress hormones such as CRH, ACTH, and cortisol.[71]

I remember my sister being so stressed out at one point in her life that she broke out in hives. We can break out with acne too. As we have seen, chronic stress leads to inflammation. With our reduced ability to regulate inflammatory responses, we see the effects on our skin. During a time when I was not managing my stress well, I began to develop rosacea. I cannot definitively say stress caused the condition, but it certainly causes flare ups. I may have already been developing the condition, and the chronic stress triggered it to surface.

There is an equivalent of the HPA axis within the hair follicle and a brain-skin axis that is influenced by chronic stress.[72]

Previously, my hair has fallen out an alarming rate when under extreme stress. I feared I was going bald. I was distressed to see the amount of hair in the shower drain each day. One study confirmed "there is a strong relationship between stress and hair loss."[73]

There are amazing interconnected systems at work in our bodies. When we do not manage stress, we throw these systems out of balance. This lack of balance can lead to some pretty concerning outcomes for our health. If you recognize some of what has been described in this chapter in your own experiences, try not to be alarmed. Instead take the gentle nudge toward embracing the importance of self-care.

CHAPTER 3

The Mental, Emotional, and Behavioral Impact of Burnout from Stress

In the last chapter, I looked at how stress impacts our bodies and all the complex processes that take place inside of us. Unmanaged stress can lead to serious physical ailments, and this chapter will touch on the mental, emotional, and behavioral impacts. Ultimately, if we want to recover, we need to handle all of these areas with care. Recognizing what is going on helps us to know what changes we need to make for our own benefit.

Effects on Our Brain

When the brain is continuously in a state of chronic stress and sending signals for cortisol release, overall brain function may be altered as time goes on. One research article noted five ways our brains are altered by stress:

1. Chronic stress increases mental disorders
2. Stress changes the brain's structure
3. Stress kills brain cells
4. Stress shrinks the brain
5. Stress hurts your memory[74]

The outcomes of chronic stress can lead to a variety of difficulties, including poor memory, sleep difficulties, moodiness, and the use of substances to help relieve that stress, such as cigarettes or alcohol. In a study of 120 students, the respondents reported having poor concentration, anxiety, anger, moodiness, decreased alertness, tendency toward social isolation, and memory problems as the top issues experienced when stressed.[75]

Chronic stress impacts our mental health. UC Berkeley researchers were also able to show that chronic stress changes the brain and how that may lead to mental issues.[76] This supports not only the study of the students who felt anxiety, anger, and moodiness, but also what I have experienced.

Working in a cubicle leaves us vulnerable to sounds that break our concentration. When stressed, I was regularly irritated when people would talk too loudly or make annoying sounds. One coworker used his computer mouse directly on the hard surface of his desk. Rather than roll it, he would pick it up and set it down repeatedly as he scrolled. I finally asked that a mouse pad be ordered for him in the next batch of office supplies. I was getting close to snapping!

In addition to irritability, brain fog and struggling to focus and remember things are common with chronic stress. During the height of my burnout, I struggled to focus on what I needed to do and would frequently forget things. I had to make lists to keep me from dropping the ball on tasks that mattered.

Elevated cortisol levels have been linked to lower reaction times and lower levels of working memory.[77] These studies tell us is that elevated levels of cortisol affect cognitive functioning. Personally I found as time went on, my ability to think on my feet had slowed down. I simply did not feel as sharp as I had once felt. I remember thinking that I was too young to be like this. I became quite concerned about these changes.

Certain areas of the brain are sensitive to high levels of stress, leaving us vulnerable to diseases related to brain function as we age.[78] One interesting thing I learned about my own brain after a brain scan was that one part of my brain was not communicating effectively with another part. This was the result of going through a time of extremely high levels of stress unrelated to work. It shows the physical and mental toll that occurs when stress is very high and chronic.

Increased cortisol may lead to late-life cognitive decline and risk for dementia due to Alzheimer's Disease.[79] We all have cortisol in our systems, and it is normal to find varying levels depending on the time of day. Remember, cortisol in and of itself is not a bad thing. Excess cortisol is the problem. Researchers have begun to focus on the difference in cortisol levels of healthy subjects versus those with a variety of health issues. Patients with dementia or mild cognitive impairment from Alzheimer's Disease have elevated cortisol levels overall.[80]

If we do not protect ourselves against the damage that stress can do to the brain, we may find ourselves vulnerable to neurodegeneration. I am not suggesting we are doomed to be diagnosed with depression or other cognitive issues like Alzheimer's. By recognizing the symptoms of chronic stress, we have the opportunity to make changes to improve our outlook. The daily struggle with memory, concentration, and moodiness only exacerbates stress. During my periods of burnout, I would panic because I was forgetting things. I felt irritated and overwhelmed by having my concentration broken by the sounds of coworkers. My reactions to things were simply an overreaction due to the stress.

The Importance of Sleep

Good quality sleep is important for recovery. We need to be able to recharge and replenish in order to have the adequate levels of energy to meet the demands of the next day. Sleep is a resource to you as well. Do not think that the only resources are the ones you get from your boss at work. You are responsible for the personal resources that help you manage the demands of your job. My hope is that you take the need for adequate sleep seriously. Sometimes it seems like our society runs on sleep deprivation and energy drinks.

I came across a study that linked burnout with specific biological markers and sleep disturbances for those experiencing chronic job strain. As mentioned before, chronic job strain has to do with high demands and low levels of control on the job. Individuals with burnout showed significantly more issues with sleep in the forms of insomnia, sleep fragmentation, and non-restorative sleep.[81] This can be due to stress keeping us awake with our minds racing but may also be due to effects of cortisol. Sleep is regulated by the HPA axis. As we have seen, when this is in a state of dysregulation, there are negative consequences.

Additionally, HbA1C is highly associated with burnout and insomnia.[82] The HbA1C test shows your three-month average of hemoglobin blood sugar levels. This test is the one used to diagnose pre-diabetes and diabetes. Additionally, the test is used to help people with those conditions manage their disease by knowing their levels. I had this test a few times when working with a doctor for weight loss. During times of chronic stress, my levels have been high. At one point, I was considered pre-diabetic. The link between the core burnout symptom of exhaustion, insomnia, and HBA1C is significant because exhaustion is the first symptom many of us experience, and this can be our warning sign in the future as we work to get into recovery and stay there.[83] It is important to understand the link between stress, poor sleep, elevated blood sugar levels, and ultimately the exhaustion we feel. Sleep is just as important as what foods you eat.

The measures of C-reactive protein (an inflammatory marker), total cholesterol, and lower concentrations of vitamin D3 for those with poor sleep are also of particular note.[84] For a period of time, I was prescribed Vitamin D3 due to my low levels. I never knew you could get so low on a vitamin that a doctor would prescribe it. Vitamin D3 is important for calcium absorption, which affects our bones, energy levels, intestinal issues, muscle pain, mood, and headaches.[85] At the time I was not told about was the importance of sleep and its relationship to Vitamin D3.

Earlier in the section on the cardiovascular system, I mentioned the presence of C-reactive protein levels being a predictor for risk of heart attack and stroke, with additional links to high cholesterol and high blood sugars. Poor sleep quality and sleep deprivation are independently associated with higher levels of high sensitivity C-reactive protein.[86] We need to prioritize getting restorative sleep to maintain our health and well-being. Who knew that a lack of quality sleep on a consistent basis could lead to these kinds of issues? I know I did not!

Our circadian rhythm is our internal body clock. Our hypothalamus helps to synchronize a 24-hour circadian rhythm. Cortisol levels follow a similar circadian rhythm. Remember the HPA axis starts with the hypothalamus. We have all heard someone say they are not a "morning person." What they are describing is their chronotype—the time of day they feel they function best. Disruption of our circadian rhythm has been shown to contribute to obesity and diabetes.[87]

Unfortunately, night shift workers are greatly impacted by this. For those having to work and sleep outside of the normal circadian rhythm, I suggest making sure you are eating for your health, getting exercise, and keeping a routine sleep schedule to the best of your ability. Doing these things can help mitigate some of the impact. Rotating shifts are not ideal; a fixed schedule is the lesser of the two evils when it comes to working night shifts.

Sleep is also important for how well our memory works. Cortisol impacts more than just working memory. We dream during rapid eye movement (REM) sleep, and non-REM sleep stages take place prior to REM sleep. Slow delta waves take place during non-REM stages 3 and 4. Studies indicate that slow wave sleep and REM sleep play a role in consolidating newly acquired information in our memory.[88]

Lack of sleep compounds the issues we have with stress, job strain, and burnout. However, we often do not make the best choices when it comes to dealing with stress. Sometimes we create a vicious cycle with the choices we make. These choices can work against us, but thankfully we have control over our choices.

Behavioral Implications of Poor Stress Management

Poor stress management shows itself in many ways in our lives. We have already reviewed how stress eating due to cortisol leads to subsequent health issues of increased BMI and visceral fat.

Other unhealthy ways we cope with stress may include smoking, using alcohol, abusing other substances, losing our temper easily, being aggressive while driving, chewing our fingernails, zoning out to TV, gaming, or obsessing over social media. These are the kinds of coping mechanisms typically noted in those who are neurotic, one of the five personality types prone to burnout. They are avoidance behaviors, and none of these will work to help us truly feel better.

I will not spend time on the health impacts of smoking or alcohol/substance use, as there are many other resources available on those topics. I do want to share about the negative impacts of some seemingly innocuous habits.

Mobile phone use at bedtime is one of those choices with a negative impact. The short wavelength light that comes from phone screens has been shown to suppress the production of melatonin, a hormone that helps prepare the body for sleep.[89] Melatonin helps with falling to sleep, staying asleep, and having better quality sleep. Many people use melatonin supplements to help with their sleep, though we may be able to naturally increase our melatonin by putting our phones away at night. Bedtime mobile phone use has been linked to poorer sleep quality, insomnia, and fatigue.[90]

When we are tired and want a little pick me up, we may tend to reach for soft drinks or energy drinks for the caffeine and sugar boost. One study found that energy drinks with both sucrose and caffeine may promote emotional alterations and brain changes.[91] If you are having anxiety issues, soft drinks or energy drinks will only exacerbate the problem. Caffeine is commonly known to cause jitteriness when we consume too much. There are healthier options for dealing with fatigue, which I will cover in chapter five.

During my periods of burnout, I frequently ate lunch at my desk while continuing to work through my lunch break. I thought I would feel better by getting ahead of the work demands or catching up on personal things, like studying, because of time constraints. One interesting study found that eating while working on a computer affected our ability to determine satiety after eating.[92] Again, stress eating was already a problem, but if I could not recognize I was full after eating lunch, this led to snacking in the afternoon. This is a type of mindless eating, similar to when we eat in front of the TV. I never saw it this way because I was working and alert, or so I thought.

Smoking, using substances, eating, drinking caffeinated beverages, and zoning out on our mobile phones, may seem like easy, momentary relief from stress, but they actually contribute to more issues in the long run. These behaviors do not alleviate the issues we are having due to high job demands, stress, and the subsequent burnout. We need to directly address the issues of exhaustion and the thoughts and emotions we carry with us each day in an effective manner in order to change.

Now that we have looked at all the negative effects of burnout and chronic stress, let us move forward to positive actions that will help you take control of your recovery.

You have the power to do this. All the suggestions that follow are relatively easy and generate positive feelings. You have already taken the first step by reading this book!

SECTION 2

Recovery For The Body

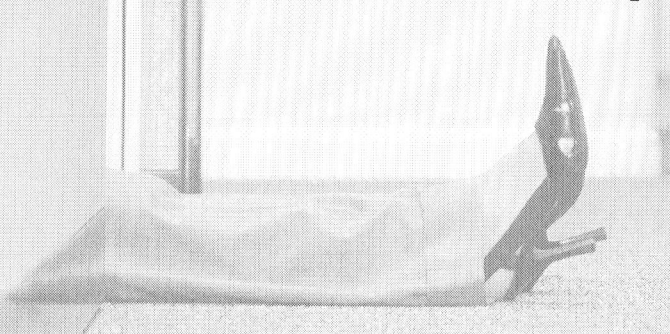

CHAPTER 4
Get Your Zzzs

We go through this life in one body. It is our ride from the day we are born until the very end. No one wants to go through life in a beat-up, busted down ride. Exhaustion takes a toll on the body, and it is a hallmark characteristic of burnout. It is hard to deal with the ongoing demands in the workplace when we are exhausted. When I was exhausted, I could not focus, and my moods fluctuated between irritability and choking back tears from sadness and feeling overwhelmed.

If you recognize symptoms from the last two chapters in your own life, you may feel like a hot mess at this point! Not to worry, my friend, because there are things well within your control to help you recover. We have the power to improve our energy levels by focusing on sleep, nutrition, and exercise. By the time you implement these strategies on a consistent basis, you might feel better than you did prior to burnout.

One thing I need to make clear is that I am not a medical doctor, nurse, or a registered dietician. My health suggestions are based on my own personal experiences and supported by research. Please always discuss your health with your physician and consult with him or her before starting any exercise or dietary programs. My suggestions worked for me, but I do not have complicated health conditions. I want to point this out up front because if you do have compounding health issues, you should always seek proper medical advice.

Good Night, Sleep Tight

Exhaustion can be both emotional and physical. Often this is due to the levels of stress and the physiological impact shared in the prior chapters. Not getting enough sleep is often a key factor leading to exhaustion.

When we are not managing stress, it is easy to develop poor sleep habits. As I mentioned before, we may resort to the use of alcohol or other drugs to deal with stress. We get caught in a vicious cycle of stress, lack of sleep, and use of energy drinks or excessive amounts to caffeine to seek some relief from being so tired. Then at night, when stress is keeping us awake due to our minds racing, we pick up cell phones and scroll through social media. That blue light then begins to have an impact on our melatonin production.

Sleep helps to restore our immune and endocrine systems, along with supporting learning, memory, and synaptic plasticity in the brain.[93] Developing good habits around sleep are critical to self-care. When we are all over the place with erratic schedules, it is hard to find our center. We need routines to help us maintain a sense of mastery over our lives. Many equate routine with boredom, but it does not have to be that way. Routines help give us structure, and within that structure we can have variety. Routines do not have to be rigid and monotonous. Try to keep an open, flexible mind about what is proposed in this chapter. You may immediately think some of these suggestions will not work for you. You may have other reasons for not trying something. The first thing I am going to get out of the way right now is to ask you to put down that darn cell phone!

You cannot truly relax if you are endlessly connected to your phone. This may mean not taking any more work calls past a certain time, not answering any more emails before bed, and certainly getting off the social media sites. Our world has trained us to believe we have to be plugged in and connected at all times or we will miss out on something. I promise you that you will not. Watching videos of someone holding a stack of signs, slowly dropping one at a time to share a story, is a waste of our precious time.

Time is the one thing we spend that we can never get back. We can spend money and earn more, but once an hour is gone, it is gone forever. You do not get a do over on that block of time. Is your health really worth that extra hour on your cell phone? You need that hour for some self-care instead.

I remember a period of time when I only slept about three hours per night. When I was struggling with insomnia, I would make the mistake of getting on my cell phone to kill some time, hoping to get sleepy again. Guess what? I rarely went back to sleep. If I finally did fall back to sleep, it was right as the alarm was going off. That taught me a valuable lesson on the impact of sleep deprivation.

Nocturnal blue light impacts neurophysiological functions. Blue light exposure during times when it is normally dark, including light from cell phones, backlit computers, and televisions, delays sleep onset, affects sleep quality, and impacts working memory and processing speed.[94] Insomnia leads to not only a constant state of fatigue, but can affect health issues of weight gain, increased insulin, and metabolic syndrome. People who engaged in a one-week intervention that blocked blue light for two hours before bedtime found improvements in their insomnia.[95] Addressing insomnia is critical for your recovery.

One study reviewed whether pharmaceutical protocols or establishing routines were better for resolving sleep issues. The results of their study indicated that setting positive bedtime routines was better than the use of drugs.[96]

Many factors can affect our sleep quality. Fortunately, there are easy things we can do to create the optimal setting for a good night's sleep.

The Mayo Clinic recommends the following actions to support better sleep:

1. Stick to a sleep schedule
2. Watch what you eat
3. Create a restful environment
4. Limit daytime naps
5. Add physical activity to your daily routine
6. Manage your worries [97]

As mentioned, our bodies are on a 24-hour circadian rhythm, which drives the sleep-wake cycle. When we stick to a routine, we help regulate that sleep-wake cycle.[98] I noticed when I became more routine with my bedtime and wake time, I began to fall asleep faster at night and would begin to naturally wake up right when my alarm was set to go off.

What we feed ourselves matters. I am not saying anything earth shattering with that statement. However, it is amazing how many of us know the importance of healthy foods but do not think about it when we make food choices. We go by cravings or what looks good in the moment instead. We all have heard to avoid caffeine and other stimulants late in the day to prevent trouble sleeping. Late night snacking can lead to heartburn for some as well.

There are foods that can actually help us sleep better. Some foods contain melatonin, along with serotonin and tryptophan, which are also known to help with sleep. While taking melatonin supplements can have some adverse effects if taken in high doses, adverse effects have not been observed when eating foods containing melatonin.[99] "Food rich in melatonin can help improve insomnia while also getting the benefit of the antioxidant, anti-inflammatory, and immune protection properties of melatonin. They include: Eggs, Fish, Mushrooms, Nuts, and Germinated legumes."[100]

As part of a nighttime routine, we can incorporate some drinks to help us sleep. You may have heard about the old home remedy of drinking warm milk to help you sleep. Milk contains tryptophan, which supports this assertion. On Thanksgiving, we often eat turkey, which is known to contain tryptophan that may lead to the after-meal sleepiness.

Tart cherries are a food of particular interest. Tart cherries have high concentrations of melatonin, which also provides antioxidant and anti-inflammatory properties.[101] Adding tart cherries to a morning smoothie is an easy way to incorporate them in your diet. Tart cherries can be found in the freezer section of your grocery store. Simply thaw out a few to add in with protein shake mix or other fruits like banana. You can also juice tart cherries for a nighttime drink. In one study, drinking eight ounces of tart cherry juice twice a day reduced insomnia for a group of research participants.[102]

A variety of teas can help as well, including *Tilia* and lemongrass tea, decaffeinated green tea, organic rooibos tea, and valerian tea.[103]

Kiwifruit was another food studied for its ability to help with insomnia and quality of sleep. "Kiwifruit is found to have a positive impact on sleep quality in terms of sleep duration and sleep efficiency. Kiwifruit has twice the serotonin levels as tomatoes and is rich in folate. This has importance because insomnia is known to be a secondary condition of folate deficiency."[104]

Relaxation and Rituals

In addition to wise food choices to help us get better sleep, we can also take action to help us reach a place of calm before bed. This is where a nighttime ritual can help. More than the routine of brushing our teeth each night before bed, we can use activities that bring about relaxation and enjoyment to build healthier habits. Soaking in the tub, stretching, using aromatherapy candles or oils, listening to relaxing music, reading, or meditating all help to relax and calm us.

One review of research studies found that music characterized as sedative or calming may improve sleep quality for those experiencing insomnia.[105] There are many options on the market for accessing this kind of music on a variety of devices. Whatever you use, consider avoiding screens that would emit blue light.

I personally became a big fan of aromatherapy about thirty years ago, when spas began scenting treatment rooms. Essential oils have been around for centuries, and recent research helps us understand more about their benefits. The use of rose oil (Rosa damascena) is effective in helping children with sleep disorders sleep better.[106] Lavender (Lavandula angustifolia) is another popular oil that is often used for its calming effects. It, too, was found to help improve sleep quality in a study with patients receiving dialysis as a safe and non-invasive option.[107]

If you are not familiar with essential oils and unsure of what to try, this list of essential oils and their known uses might help. William Setzer, with the Department of Chemistry at the University of Alabama in Huntsville, listed the following oils as having calming effects or possibly reducing anxiety:[108]

- Roman chamomile
- Ylang-ylang

- Neroli
- Bergamot
- Rose geranium
- Sandalwood
- Lemon balm
- Lemon verbena

I would not suggest ingesting the oils. Please read the labels on any that you purchase to know if direct application to your skin is advised or not. Some directions may suggest applying to a cotton ball and simply smelling the scent.

Meditation has long been known to reduce stress. Many people think of meditation as the deep trance that yogis in India practice, but there are other meditative forms that are easy for any of us to practice. Meditation has many positive impacts, including regulating the HPA axis to help with cortisol levels, increasing melatonin levels, regulating blood flow to executive regions of the brain during sleep, and bringing about a relaxation response.[109]

If you are not familiar with meditation or have little experience with it, do not worry. Simply focusing on your breathing is an easy way to begin a meditative practice. Put your attention on your breathing and count to four as you inhale, then count to four as you exhale. Continue rounds of this practice until you feel calmer. This helps you to slow your breathing and increase your awareness of deep breathing verses shallow chest breathing.

Some other options include listening to a pre-recorded guided meditation. Please visit my coaching website at www.revealedpotential.com for a free companion workbook that shares more about meditation, breathing, and other ways you can put into action what you are learning here.

As part of self-care, I encourage you to get massages periodically. Most locations now have certified massage therapists. Massages not only help us relax, but they are known to help with blood circulation and releasing tight muscles and knots. If you regularly have aches in the neck, shoulders, and upper and lower back, you may be carrying too much tension from stress. There are also many options for massage equipment you can use yourself, including handheld devices, chair cushions, and large reclining massage chairs. Whatever method you choose, the important thing is releasing the tension from your muscles.

Progressive muscle relaxation is a mental and physical technique that directs you to mentally scan your body while squeezing and releasing muscles in progression. Normally you work from head to toe or toe to head. For example, lie on your back and breathe in slowly and deeply a few times. Focus on your toes and feet, and curl toes tight as you breathe in on a count of four. Exhale on a count of four as you allow the toes and foot to relax. Next, focus on your calf muscles, breathing in as you flex calf muscles and relaxing them as you breathe out. Continue all around your body, moving to your thighs, buttocks, stomach, fingers, hands, arms, shoulders, chest, neck, jaw, and forehead.

I personally have found progressive muscle relaxation to work for me when I have anxiety and cannot sleep. I learned about this years ago when I was an addictions counselor. We introduced clients to this technique as a healthy way to manage stress.

As mentioned earlier, we need to manage our worries so they do not impact our sleep. Addressing anxiety is an important aspect of recovery from burnout, which we will examine more in the next section of the book. For now, some simple practices of journaling might help keep you from spinning things around in your head most of the night. I suggest journaling about an hour before bed and not right at bedtime. This gives you time to empty your thoughts on paper and then move on to other relaxing rituals before you try to sleep, allowing for your journaled feelings and thoughts to subside.

Begin to practice some of these bedtime routines as you begin your recovery. Power down from electronics at least a couple of hours before bed. Incorporate melatonin-producing foods throughout your day. Allow yourself some time to wind down as you end your day. Soak in a bath, practice deep breathing, and empty your thoughts into a journal. You do not need to hold racing thoughts in your head all night long. We touched a bit on nutrition in this chapter on sleep. The next chapter will address the foods that can help us in our recovery from exhaustion and mental stress in more depth.

CHAPTER 5

Nutrition to Beat Exhaustion

What we eat truly matters. A healthy diet helps with our sleep and our energy levels. One thing I noticed at the peak of my burnout was exhaustion with brain fog. I just did not feel like I could think clearly or quickly. I was easily confused or had trouble staying focused. It was very frustrating at times.

I had a personal goal that required me to have a good memory, however, I could not focus or remember well enough to complete it. I was participating in a speaker's bootcamp for three days. After day one, we were tasked with putting the final touches on what we would speak about for a professional video recording the next day. I stayed up most of the night trying to remember what I wanted to say even though I had practiced it before showing up for this training, as I knew what to expect.

My frustration grew because it was my own story. How could I not remember what I wanted to say about my own story? My speech needed to cover key points and flow in a coherent manner, and those aspects tripped me up. After getting very little sleep and endless attempts to practice, I still struggled to remember without freezing up. I sat down and cried. I started this training during a time when I was deep in burnout, exhausted, stressed, and becoming very depressed. I packed up my hotel room and checked out before the start of day two; I simply walked away after spending a substantial amount of money to be there! I felt completely defeated. I had never done such a thing before.

I knew I could not allow this to continue if I wanted to reach my personal goals. I started looking into what I could do to improve my memory. I came across the Superbrain series by Jim Kwik on Mindvalley.[110] He described walnuts and blueberries as brain food. It was the first time I actually considered that foods could help with my memory. I strongly encourage you to check out his excellent program.

Once I became aware that blueberries and walnuts were good for my brain, I was curious about other foods that could be beneficial. In my review of research on stress, the brain, and nutrition, several studies found connections between certain foods and how they appeared to support neural functioning.

Oxidative stress has been shown to be related to the damage of neural structures in the brain.[111] In a prior chapter we covered stress and its effect on the brain, looking at how unmanaged stress leads to excess cortisol in our bodies. That excess cortisol can lead to oxidative stress, which impacts how our organs function. Studies have shown that fruits and nuts are beneficial for brain functioning and protection.

In order to counteract oxidative stress, we need antioxidants in our diet. Berries, including blueberries, cranberries, blackberries, and strawberries, reduce oxidative stress and neuroinflammation.[112] Incorporate berries daily by adding them to your cereal or yogurt in the morning, making a fruit smoothie, adding them to a lunch salad, or enjoying fruit as your dessert. There are many great recipes found on the internet to inspire you to add berries to your diet. I eat half a cup of blueberries each day with my Greek yogurt. I can honestly say that since I began my daily intake of blueberries, I have noticed an improvement in my memory.

Polyphenols are the beneficial micronutrients found in berries and grapes. Polyphenols found in blueberries and grapes were used in studies to measure the improvement found in adults with cognitive impairment. The use of blueberry juice once a day for three months indicated improvement for memory in older adults with early memory decline.[113]

There are thousands of polyphenols found in a variety of fruits and vegetables. Flavonoids are the most common type of polyphenol. One type of flavonoid is anthocyanin, which gives berries and grapes their color from red orange to blue violet. This is why you are encouraged to "eat the rainbow" each day. When you eat a variety of fruits and vegetables, you can be confident you are gaining the benefits of these properties. One set of researchers drew the conclusion that clinical research supports "the beneficial influence of berry intake for overall brain health and cognitive performance."[114]

Resveratrol is another polyphenol unique to grapes and red wine. Concord grapes were also put to the test. Another study found that supplementing the diet of older adults with early memory decline showed improvement in memory function with regular consumption of 100% Concord grape juice.[115]

Other foods are noted to have benefits as well. Foods like broccoli, asparagus, carrots, spinach, and artichokes also have polyphenols. One study divided foods into four groups: fruit, vegetable, legumes, and juices. Middle-aged participants with a higher intake of mushrooms, cabbage, and nuts had better cognitive function at baseline compared to those with less intake. Five years later they found those with higher overall intake of vegetables, cabbage, or other root vegetables had less decline in cognitive function. Generally, they stated that eating cabbage, nuts, and root vegetables may help diminish age related cognitive decline for those who are middle age.[116]

As mentioned already, nuts have many beneficial properties. In particular, walnut consumption was connected to improved critical thinking and inference in young adults.[117] Being able to think critically in your career or in school matters a great deal. If we are unable to hear information or read pertinent data and draw appropriate conclusions, it can lead to poor performance. Being on your game and feeling sharp helps you feel empowered.

Omega 3 fatty acids offer health benefits as well. There are commercials all the time for supplements that are available at your local pharmacy or grocery, and a growing body of evidence supports how beneficial it is to have sufficient amounts of Omega 3 fatty acids. Omega 3 fatty acids include DHA and EPA. Our bodies do not produce these, so we have to get them from either a food source or through supplements. DHA is known for aiding brain development, and EPA is known to help reduce inflammation. With some younger adults, supplementation with Omega 3 was found to have a stabilizing effect on anger and confusion. In middle age it was found to have positive effects on memory function, and some older adults showed heightened neuronal response.[118]

Omega 3 fatty acids can be found in a variety of foods in addition to supplements. EPA and DHA are found in fish such as mackerel, salmon, oysters, herring, and other Omega 3 fatty acids are also in flax seeds, chia seeds, and our friend the walnut.[119]

On my own nutritional journey, I wanted to know what energy enhancing foods to reach for instead of my usual junk food when I needed a boost. I also was curious about caffeine, since it often gets a bad rap in general. I love coffee, and I wanted to know if I should be more mindful about my intake. I found that moderate use of caffeine, at no more than 200 mg at one time, or no more than 400 mg over the course of the day, was not found to have any harmful effects for our health.[120] So, it is okay to still enjoy your favorite coffee or tea each day. Just be aware of how much you are taking in and be sure to drink water as well. Water is excellent for hydration. Every plan for healthy eating I have reviewed advises staying hydrated to avoid false hunger. We have to get that managed if we are stress eating.

For other foods to reach for when you are in a bit of a slump, registered dieticians advise eating bananas; lean proteins like chicken, turkey or salmon; nuts, including almonds, walnuts, and cashews; eggs; and apples. Drinking water is also highly encouraged.[121]

I can vouch for the bananas personally. I have found they are always given out in the half marathons around mile eight of the race. They always helped give me energy when I was lagging. One study on cyclists and the use of bananas for energy found that eating bananas before and during prolonged and intensive exercise was an effective way to fuel up and support performance.[122]

As you can see, we can find easy and healthier ways to give ourselves energy and improve mental clarity. Rather than continuing an unhealthy cycle of excessive use of energy drinks, fatty foods, and other poor-quality choices that lead to energy crashes, we can begin to make small and effective changes so we can sleep better, lose the mind fog, and combat oxidative stress.

Cravings can be difficult to manage. Trust me, I have struggled with those myself. I have learned from experience that the cravings may be caused by:

- Not getting enough sleep
- Not drinking enough water
- Letting yourself get too hungry or not eating on a regular schedule
- Eating refined sugars (fuels that sugar addiction)

- Not managing stress
- Succumbing to habits at a certain time of day

Cravings can be overcome by planning ahead. Keep healthy snacks ready and available, drink eight ounces of water throughout the day, or go for a brisk walk. If habits are a problem, you may need to replace your prior habit with a new habit. Keep a journal of what is going on when you feel cravings. Are you stressed? Did you skip a meal? Have you had enough water? You can make simple notes in a notebook to help you identify the triggers. Once you know your personal triggers, you can develop a plan of attack against the cravings. Sometimes our triggers are social, like a coworker wanting to take a coffee break together to eat sticky buns. You may need to ask your coworker to take a walk with you instead as part of the new habit.

Speaking of walking, as we recover, we need to implement exercise into our routines. We have touched on the areas of sleep and nutrition. Stick with me in chapter six for ideas of what exercise you can easily incorporate in your life to benefit your health. The goal here is to reduce stress and feel your energy levels return.

At this point, you may be wondering if any of this really works. I was able return and successfully complete the speaker training I mentioned at the beginning of this chapter. I had the energy I needed to focus, maintain clarity, and best of all remember what I wanted to say! I attribute this to changing my diet. I no longer experienced exhaustion and mental confusion. Addressing this area of my burnout allowed me to pick back up where I left off on my personal goals. Additionally, it supported the next area of burnout recovery, incorporating exercise.

CHAPTER 6

Exercise Away Your Stress

I have good news for you, my friend! This chapter on exercise will put a smile on your face. I found studies that show you do not have to survive a boot camp every single day to gain the benefits of exercise. Yippee!! Now I like to be outside and run, but that habit developed over time. I spent thirty years telling myself how much I hated running. I was a couch potato for at least two decades before embracing the benefits of exercise.

We now know that oxidative stress impacts the brain and the body in a harmful way. As we age, this happens naturally, but unmanaged stress, poor nutrition, poor sleep, and a sedentary lifestyle compound those stressors, leading to negative outcomes. You can make changes, regardless of your age, and still see benefits. It is not too late. Even sedentary older adults benefit from merely walking consistently to see improvement in brain function.[123] If you are still young, a different trajectory can begin right now, and your future self will thank you. Even if you are in middle age, your future self will be grateful for this course correction in your life.

Simply going for an enjoyable walk at an easy pace can lead to benefits. Again, you do not have to survive an intensive workout to get benefits. Just one mile at an easy to moderate pace was found to be sufficient enough to capitalize on the brain's plasticity and improve brain health.[124] When we walk, we can lower our stress levels. Anything repetitive in nature tends be calming.

One in-depth review of clinical studies on oxidative stress concluded the following about the benefits of exercise:

- Helps increase energy expenditure and reduce visceral fat
- Increases nutritive blood supply to skeletal muscles and removes waste from them as well
- Improves the immune system response by reducing inflammation
- Reduces the incidences of diseases associated with oxidative stress
- Enhances the cellular repair process [125]

Not only are we enhancing our brain function when we exercise, we can see other benefits as well. I feel better when I exercise. As I am writing this section, I am recovering from foot surgery. I have not gone for a run in two weeks. I did squeeze in one more half marathon three days before surgery so that I was "trained up" because I knew I was going into a period of being sedentary. I can tell you that I do not feel like myself right now. I have found a deep appreciation for being active because of how good I feel compared to when I am sedentary. Years ago, I was overweight and sedentary. I fully understand what that is like and pass no judgement on anyone. If you are struggling with that right now, please know you are not alone. Please also know that this state is temporary depending on what you decide to do. It is in your control to make changes with your choices. I hope you choose to invest in your future self and prevent the health risks associated with a sedentary lifestyle.

Prolonged sedentary behaviors have a connection with insomnia and sleep difficulties.[126] Watching TV and spending time on phones, tablets, and laptops go hand in hand with sedentary behavior. As previously mentioned, the light given off these devices affects melatonin production, which is then linked to sleep issues. You may think you are relaxing during these sedentary times, but in reality, you may be compounding other issues. Simply getting extra sleep rather than being sedentary watching television will make a difference. Exchanging about thirty minutes of sedentary time for additional sleep and moderate to vigorous physical activity helps to improve executive functioning in the brain.[127] Being sedentary is not the same as getting restorative sleep, and it will harm you in the long run. Get your restorative sleep, but also get moving!

I briefly touched on meditation and progressive muscle relaxation in the section on developing sleep rituals. Some other gentle but effective ways to reduce stress include meditative movement, including tai chi, qigong, and yoga. Around ten years ago I was in China watching an early morning group practice tai chi at a local park. As they moved through their poses in unison, each person seemed to be in a peaceful flow. I felt at peace simply watching them glide from one position to the next.

A review of various studies found that both tai chi and qigong demonstrated similar outcomes for lowering blood pressure, improving mental health by elevating mood and reducing anger, and improving functional balance and improving immune functions.[128] As a former yoga instructor, I can personally attest to the calm I feel while practicing yoga. Even as the instructor while paying attention to the needs of my students, I still felt a sense of calm despite not being able to only focus on my own yoga poses. The breath work involved in yoga and simply being in the moment holding a pose both allow stress to dissipate. One study found that yoga could reduce stress in as little as thirty minutes.[129]

To reduce stress while at work, you can actually practice chair-based yoga. This makes it easy and convenient for you to bring your stress levels down without having to pack a gym bag and fight traffic to get to a class after work. If you are wondering if this is as effective as going to a yoga class, one study indicated it was. The study focused on performing chair-based yoga postures or a guided meditation at your desk for fifteen minutes to see if it would be effective at lowering stress levels. The study found that both resulted in a reduction of perceived stress and in physiological markers of stress.[130] You can find a chair-based yoga sequence in the workbook available to download at www.revealedpotential.com.

To make exercise more fun, look for options that appeal to you. See if there are any groups meeting for a particular kind of recreation you enjoy. Groups of people meet to walk, run, kayak, hike trails, practice yoga, lift weights, and engage in other forms of recreation. Allowing exercise to become more of a social outing certainly can make it more fun; that was my experience with running. I had a 5K as a bucket list goal and found a group meeting for a couch to 5K program. I made new friends and ended up developing a lifestyle that included running half marathons. I stopped hating running because I chose to turn it into something fun. I travel to new cities to run races now. Plus, I learned about interval running, allowing me to take walk breaks. That helped me out a bunch!

So many of our lifestyle choices are intertwined. Our choices to spend excessive time on smart phones, eat poorly, and remain sedentary will lead to poor quality sleep, which then leads to feeling exhausted and having brain fog. We cannot deal with the demands of our jobs under these conditions. We then begin the vicious cycle of looking for energy in quick-fix energy drinks, excessive amounts of coffee, sugars, and other unhealthy foods. We spark cravings and often have trouble managing our stress-related eating. This vicious downward spiral ultimately contributes to burnout.

I hope you can see how easy it is to make small adjustments in each of these areas to begin to enjoy the health benefits. Change does not require a major life overhaul. Add some blueberries to your morning yogurt. Go for a walk on your lunch hour. Turn off your electronics a couple of hours before bed and simply focus on your breathing to relax. Pick one thing and implement it consistently. Then add the next thing that appeals to you. This is the beginning of your recovery.

Sometimes when we begin to adjust our diet and exercise, we can slip into "New Year's resolution" mode. We can make grandiose plans of what we will do with our diet and exercise, then about a week later, life happens, and we get thrown off track. As regular life stressors occur again and again, our plans may be tossed by the wayside completely.

Do not view your burnout recovery like a New Year's resolution. Please stay in this moment, today. What will you do today that is good for you? What are one or two easy changes you can choose to make today? If you have an off day, do not allow it to throw you off track. Just choose to be good to yourself the next day. Get in the habit of noticing when you choose to be good to yourself.

Often it is easier to add a good habit to your day than to remove a bad habit. Do not focus on all the things you see yourself as doing wrong. Recovery is not about chastisement or punishment. Recovery is about self-care. Pick one thing that appeals to you and choose to implement it daily until it becomes a healthy habit. As time goes on, you will find you are adding more healthy choices to your day and feeling more energy.

SECTION 3

Recovery For The Mind

CHAPTER 7

Change Your Thinking to Change Your Life

In this section of the book, we will focus on being more aware of our thinking and how our thoughts can lead to mental exhaustion. The previous chapters covered how sleep, diet, and exercise affect how our bodies manage physical exhaustion. Our thoughts can also drain us and add to our stress. We can address our mental exhaustion by changing how we think to enhance our resilience to the daily demands we face.

Neural Pathways

For some time now, I have heard about how our thinking affects our brains. When we think negative thoughts, neural pathways are developed, and when we think positive thoughts, different pathways are developed. We need to retrain our way of thinking to get out of burnout. Some of our natural tendencies toward negative thinking may actually stoke burnout in the first place.

Neuroscientists have discovered that our brains are wired to have a negativity bias.[131] Assuming the worst and being distrustful and on guard served us well thousands of years ago, when the world was truly full of threats to human life. In modern times, however, it does not always serve us in a way that is helpful. This negativity bias can lead us to perceive harsh criticism or high levels of social or performance demands as threatening.[132] These perceived threats are treated the same way as real threats in the body, causing the release of stress hormones. How we view the world and perceive things becomes our own reality. Someone else may perceive an experience differently and therefore have a different reality even in the same environment. How many times have you had a disagreement with another person because their viewpoint was vastly different from your own? That is the impact of perception.

Areas of our brain are activated by what we think and do. Think of your mind as your thought and information transfer. Our brains can change as our minds change, millisecond by millisecond, and the changes can be lasting.[133] The brain sends information over synapses from one neuron to another. A synapse is the space between neurons that neurotransmitter chemicals help to get information sent from one neuron to another. To quote famous Canadian psychologist Donald Hebb, "neurons that fire together, wire together."[134] Neurons that are regularly activated lead to stronger pathways, and those not activated result in weaker pathways. The brain will not put energy into preserving those. The old adage "use it or lose it" applies to neurons in our brain.[135] The wonderful thing about our brains is that they are able to change, a capability referred to as neuroplasticity. Think about instances of people overcoming serious brain injuries to walk and talk again. New learning requires the actual structure of the brain to change over time to support neuronal connections.[136]

What we think about matters. If we regularly engage in negative thinking, certain neural pathways are activated and strengthened. You want to be aware of your thinking and what you are regularly building.

Neuroscientist Rick Hanson describes what this mechanism looks like:[137]

- Increased activity leads to greater excitability of individual neurons in the brain
- Blood flow to active neuronal regions increases

- Neurons that are firing build stronger synapses
- New synapses develop among active neurons stretching toward each other

When we think positive thoughts, we build neural pathways that can reduce the release of stress hormones.

Dr. Hanson also goes on to say: "[The] mind can cause changes in matter (the material brain) through its embedding in the matter that represents it; for example, immaterial thoughts of gratitude are embodied in cascading physical processes, which can trigger physical circuits that dampen the release of stress hormones."[138]

How many times can you recall when you perceived something as a crisis and felt the stress, just as if your life depended on the outcome? I know I have perceived situations as being a big deal, which caused stress at the time. Now that I look back, I can see how I overreacted and did not keep those situations in perspective. Over time, I have learned to temper my reactions more than I did when I was younger. I now have the insight from learning about thought distortions to help me grow beyond that place of panic. Our perception of events in our daily lives can lead to stressors regardless of whether the event is truly a threat or not. When we perceive an event as potentially harmful, the fight or flight response is triggered.

Thought Distortions

On my journey to increased self-awareness and self-development, I became a certified practitioner in neurolinguistic programming. It is a model of how we communicate with ourselves and others. I am certified by the Association for Integrative Psychology and was trained under Dr. Matt James. Additionally, some of what I will be sharing with you I learned as an addictions counselor, because addicts have thought distortions that can create barriers to recovery. I believe the same is true with our recovery from burnout.

Have you ever experienced an event that you interpreted differently from others involved? You may have wondered if that other person was even in the same room or how in the world they could describe it so differently from what you experienced.

When each of us experience an event, we either distort, delete, or generalize the facts of what actually took place. We all filter events based on our points of reference, including past experiences, deeply held belief systems, values, methods of processing information, decisions, and our emotional state at the time.

When we distort information, we misrepresent reality. For example, each time I go out for an early morning run, I see a snake on the road. As I get closer, that snake is really just a twig or a piece of rope. My mind distorts the image until I get close enough to see it for what it really is.

Generalization occurs when we draw conclusions about a current event based on only one or two prior experiences. Generalizations are limiting and do not consider all the actual facts. When we generalize, we have the tendency to overestimate or underestimate.

When we delete information, we are being selective with what information we choose to receive. We pay attention to certain parts of the event and omit the rest. We typically do this when faced with too much information.

There are several ways distortions, generalizations, and deletions can show up in our thinking about events. See if you recognize any of these as you think about your current job situation.

Distortions:

- **Mind Reading** — "I just know my boss doesn't like me." This occurs any time we think we know someone else's internal thoughts and feelings. Ask yourself: How do I know this? What evidence do I have to believe this person feels or thinks this way?
- **Value Judgements** — "It will be bad if we don't get this done today." This is placing a judgment on a situation. Challenge that kind of thinking by asking the following: Why is this bad? Who says it is bad? How do I know it is bad?
- **Cause and Effect** — "Their constant mistakes make me so stressed out." This is placing the blame or root cause outside of oneself. Ask yourself the following: How am I choosing to be stressed out over someone's mistakes? Why am I choosing to internalize this? By asking these questions, you put yourself in a place of choice rather than being a victim. When you challenge faulty cause and effect distortions, you can actively choose not to react to the behaviors of others.
- **Complex Equivalent** — "He hasn't answered my emails, so I guess he doesn't care." This equates the behavior of not answering emails to whether this person cares about a particular situation. The behavior could very well be completely unrelated to the person's feelings. Ask yourself what meaning you are assigning to the situation and what facts you have to support that meaning.

Generalizations:

- **Black and White/Dichotomous Thinking** — "They never pay attention to our requests." The use of words like *always, never, everyone, no one, all,* and *every* indicate dichotomous thinking. These words generalize beyond a single event. Ask yourself the following: Does this really happen every time? Is it really everyone? How often does it actually happen?
- **Words of Necessity** — "I have to take care of this." These are words that imply we *must do, should do, have to do,* or *need to do* something. They could also indicate things we *should not* or *must not* do. Ask yourself: What will happen if I do not complete this task? Why must I do it? Why should I not do it? What would happen if I did?
- **Words of Possibility/Impossibility** — "There is no way I will pass this certification process." These are words such as *can, can't, will, won't, may, may not, possible,* and *impossible*. Ask yourself: What is preventing me from reaching my goal? What *can* I do? Why *can't* I do this or that?

Deletions:

- **Omitting Specifics** — "We have no communication here." Similar to generalizations, omitting specific details leads to dichotomous thinking. Ask yourself: Who is not communicating? What is not being communicated?
- **The Royal They** — "They don't care." Also similar to a generalization, we may refer to a nonspecific "they" in the office. This is a deletion of your specific coworkers.

Ask yourself: Who doesn't care? What don't they care about?
- **Empty Comparisons** — "She is better than I am." Comparison using words like *better, worse, most, least, more* and *less* also tends to delete specific details. We compare without any specifics to support our conclusions. Ask yourself: What is she better at? How is she better? How do I define *better* in this specific situation? Comparison is the thief of joy, my friend. Drop this one as quickly as you can!

When I worked as an addiction's counselor, we spent time helping clients understand the many ways their thinking resulted in inaccurate conclusions about themselves and others. Here are a few more examples to consider:

- **Catastrophizing** — This occurs when we take one event and imagine a chain of events spiraling out of control and ending with disaster. An example of this would be having your boss send a report back to you to correct one area, but your mind spirals out to the point that you are sure if you make one more tiny mistake, you will be fired. Look back on all the near disasters you thought you would have. Did they really actually happen? I bet most did not.
- **Selective Thinking** — When we get fixated on one point completely, we sometimes overlook any other pieces of information. Imagine giving a presentation and receiving feedback sheets at the end. All are full of positive remarks except one. The one form critiques certain portions of the presentation. Selective thinking happens when you fixate on this one critique and dismiss all the other positive remarks. You may even

feel so upset that you never want to give a presentation again.
- **Personalization** — Sometimes we take a situation that is not actually connected to us and personalize it. An example of this could be believing that you were not included on an email on purpose to sabotage you at work by making you miss out on information. Like mind reading, this attributes emotions to someone else's actions.

The mental energy spent on this catastrophizing, selective thinking, and personalization can lead to exhaustion and subsequently burnout. We can get in the mindset that others never pick up the slack, we must take care of everything or it will all fall apart, and if we do not do things just perfectly, we will be fired. What a burden to carry every day!

Take some time to see where you might be falling into some of these traps. I suggest keeping a journal and writing each day about what you are thinking and feeling. After a week, go back and reread what you wrote. You may see some of these thoughts showing up in your journal entries.

We add to our stress with how we perceive situations. In order to recover from burnout, we need to get really honest with ourselves about how we need to change our thinking in order to reduce stress and feel better. If you refuse to honestly evaluate your thoughts, I can say from personal experience you are at risk of suffering burnout again even if you quit your current job. Your mind goes with you wherever you are, and your mind creates your reality. You can keep changing the scenery, but if you have the same "stinking thinking" with you, it will spoil the new scene for you eventually. When I worked in addictions, we created relapse prevention plans that addressed stinking thinking.

We should also improve our mindset through awareness of optimistic verses pessimistic thinking. The thought spirals listed above can feed pessimistic thinking. Our thinking can lead us to feel helpless about events and circumstances. In the book *Flourish*, Dr. Martin Seligman discusses positive psychology and well-being. He found differences in thinking between those who had "learned helplessness" compared to those who did not.

Dr. Seligman shared the following:[139]

1. Those with learned helplessness saw situations as being permanent or lasting a very long time instead of being temporary.
2. Those with learned helplessness believed there was nothing they could do about the situation compared to those who believed change was possible.
3. Those with learned helplessness transferred the negative feelings into situations that were unrelated to the event taking place, for example, carrying work stress into their home life. Those with optimism saw the situation as local and did not transfer it to other areas of their life.

Fortunately, there are tools we can use to help us get our head in the game and stop making ourselves miserable by becoming victims of circumstance. We can challenge our thinking with the examples already given and a few other wonderful tools.

Reframing

One way we can learn to stop assuming the worst is to use the power for reframing. Events take place in our daily lives, and the meaning we assign to these events leads us to feel at peace or in distress. Let me say that again: It is the meaning we assign to the event, not the event itself, that causes us pain.

It is very human of us to see others as causing us pain or discomfort because of the things they say or do. I have learned over the course of my five decades on this earth that more often than not, the other person never considered me at all. Most of the time, other people are not plotting against you. Others may simply be caught up in their own circumstances. Words and actions actually reflect more on the other person than they do on you.

While still married to my first husband, I learned one valuable lesson at a retreat. This retreat was specifically designed for women whose lives were upside down due to their husbands' extramarital affairs. As you can imagine, my thoughts were all over the place, and I was struggling to make sense of everything. The point of the retreat was to take back our lives. I learned to stop giving so much power to the pain the affair had caused, to find healing, and to own my happiness once again. I am forever grateful for what I learned at that retreat because it changed my way of thinking.

The retreat leader told us that our spouses and their affair partners did not *do* anything *to us*. You may be thinking hold up, what you are you talking about? It was an awful, hurtful thing that they did. How can you say they did not do anything to you? She explained that they were so wrapped up in their own fantasy, their own thoughts and feelings, that their spouses were never even considered. It was not realistic to think they plotted to have an affair just to cause me pain. They were so wrapped up in their own issues that my feelings were never even considered. Believe it or not, simply gaining that little nugget of truth helped me tremendously.

This same lesson has applied to many situations in my life since then. It takes the sting out of the thoughtless words or behaviors of others. I give the benefit of the doubt and assume if the other person was aware of how their words and behaviors affected others, they would do it differently. Many people go through life completely unaware. Do not give so much power to other people's actions. Your irritating coworker is most likely not doing things on purpose to upset you. Reframing allows you to take back control of your perceptions and reactions.

Now, I do know that truly toxic workplaces with toxic employees exist. This book is not about surviving a toxic workplace. This book is about the typical work environment, which often contributes to burnout, along with how we compound it with our own thinking.

Specific reframing techniques help ease the upset and discomfort events may cause us. The first way to reframe a problem is by changing the meaning. For example, suppose a coworker often plays devil's advocate in meetings. This is viewed as a problem because of the meaning assigned to this behavior. If you believe the coworker does this just to be a difficult pain in the neck, of course you will be annoyed! However, what if you consider an alternative meaning? What if the coworker is concerned and looking out for the team? Maybe he wants to protect the team from problems and the resulting consequences of not considering all factors? With a different motivation, you may now see this coworker as someone who has your back, leading to positive feelings rather than annoyance. One of my favorite mentors, Paul Martinelli, teaches that we should assume noble intentions. This means giving the benefit of the doubt to the other person by assuming what he or she is doing is for noble reasons. Assuming noble intentions can quickly diffuse frustrations in many cases.

The next way to reframe is by changing the context. While I was actively in burnout, I would sigh and look at everything I needed to do for the day. I would think I could not keep up with everything because there was not enough of me to go around. We had more work and less staff to handle things, a trend that continued across fields due to the Covid pandemic. I am glad I learned how to change my thinking, or I might have easily found myself back in burnout. In all honestly, reminding myself to reframe takes effort, but changing my thinking has been important to my recovery.

Rather than seeing myself in a situation with too much to do, I changed the context to envision a situation where I could practice my prioritizing skills. I went from thinking *I am not enough* to *I can prioritize the most important things to do today, and I feel confident I can get those done.* That felt a lot less overwhelming. I did not have to do everything. What freedom! When I changed the narrative in my head from critical to praising my strengths, my prioritizing became a finely tuned skill.

What is your narrative? Do you assume the worst about others? Are you harsh and critical of yourself? Does it involve thought distortions, such as catastrophizing? Do you "should" on yourself and others? You know what I mean—I "should" do this; he "should" do that. Do not "should" on yourself or others!

All of this takes practice and raising your own awareness of what you are thinking and feeling. An effective way to begin is to take a step back. If you stay caught up in turmoil, raising your awareness will be more challenging. Our next chapter is about how stepping back and becoming mindful can be beneficial for our recovery.

CHAPTER 8

Mindfulness Matters

Mindfulness refers to "paying attention in a particular way; on purpose, in the present moment, and non-judgmentally."[140]

Mindfulness is gaining popularity in the corporate world because of the effectiveness of the practice to reduce stress. In particular, mindfulness helps protect against burnout. One study with teachers found that mindfulness had a "strong, protective effect against emotional exhaustion, depersonalization, and lower personal accomplishment,"[141] many of the hallmarks of burnout.

In high-stress moments, it is easy to fall into old habits. Those habits may include losing our temper, stuffing down the stress with junk food, or becoming overwhelmed with emotions. Practicing mindfulness allows you to take a step back from the chaos around you. You may feel like you are at a three-ring circus, but that does not mean you have to be the ringmaster. It is okay to exit the tent, even if only in your mind.

We can avoid reacting to stressors by using mindfulness. It helps increase our self-awareness. We become aware of what we are thinking and feeling in the moment. When we engage in the non-judgmental aspect of mindfulness, we increase our compassion for ourselves and others. Mindfulness can lead to greater positive emotions that reduce feelings of low personal accomplishment.[142] When we are compassionate with ourselves, we can more accurately see what we have truly accomplished instead of viewing ourselves as failures.

In one interesting study, US Marines participated in an eight-week mindfulness-based mind and fitness training. The marines who participated in the training had faster recovery of their heart rate and breathing, improved sleep, and lower levels of the hormone neuropeptide Y (NPY) after stressful combat training.[143] Mindfulness can allow us to reengage in a way that is less reactionary. The ability to lead yourself in high-stress situations without being reactionary will serve you well throughout life. The point of mindfulness is not to escape. It is to decompress and reengage from a calmer place of being.

As I mentioned, our perception of stress leads to our reactions and the consequences of unmanaged stress. Mindfulness is a fantastic and simple method to use daily to help in our recovery and prevent relapse back into burnout. Remember, I burned out more than once because I had not learned the lessons of what caused it, how to recover from it, and certainly not how to prevent it from happening again. According to Arunas Antanaitis, "[Mindfulness is a] remarkable, simple practice that rewires the brain in a way that allows individuals to become more resilient to the stressors of everyday life."[144]

Earlier I wrote about the Big Five personality traits and how a lack of being open to new experiences was often found among those who are burned out. Mindfulness helps with increasing our receptivity and interest in new experiences,[145] thanks to the non-judgmental aspect of the practice. Often the resistance to new experiences comes from having a preconceived notion of what should or should not be. This is a form of judgement. It is also a form of distorted thinking. By practicing not passing judgement on situations and simply accepting them for what they are, we begin to reduce our engagement in this thought distortion. If we are not upset about things all the time because they are not going as they should, we increase our sense of well-being.

To benefit from mindfulness, three axioms need to be present: intention, attention, and attitude.[146] Intention is the reason or purpose for practicing mindfulness. You might want to reduce stress, increase patience with coworkers, or any other purpose that helps you achieve your personal goals. Attention is simply being aware without judging thoughts or feelings. Attention includes being aware of your environment as well. Attitude is the mindset you have while practicing mindfulness. You can choose to be kind and compassionate to yourself and others. You can choose to be harsh and judgmental as well. You will only gain the benefit of mindfulness when you ditch the critical mindset.

With ongoing practice, three benefits appear. First, we gain self-regulation and self-management.[147] When we stop, breathe, and become mindful of our thoughts, feelings, and external situations, we prevent habitual reactions. This self-regulation can short circuit the unhealthy patterns we have. We can now choose how we will respond instead of simply reacting.

We also gain a greater sense of our values.[148] We become more aware of what is meaningful to us. We observe situations and become aware of the thoughts and feelings that arise. Often values are prescribed in childhood by others, and we simply follow along. Some of these "values" can lead to thought distortions when they become a filter through which we view the world. The values of the adults from our childhood may have supported unhealthy messages, such as boys do not cry and women who speak up for themselves are difficult and demanding. Some of the values you carry around may not really be your own. Mindfulness can help us clarify what is true for us so that we can choose behaviors that align with that truth.[149]

Third, we gain cognitive, emotional, and behavioral flexibility.[150] When we simply observe and are not emotionally invested in the current experience, we can learn to be more flexible in our thinking because our emotions are not in charge. We then act in ways more beneficial to our well-being. This ties back to being open to new experiences. We simply let things unfold rather than fighting against them.

There are simple ways to be mindful. First, simply pay attention to your breathing. Count your inhale for four or five breaths and count your exhale for four or five breaths. You can also pay attention to what you see, hear, touch, smell, taste, think, and feel emotionally.

Labeling a thought as a thought and a feeling as a feeling can help lead to more flexibility.[151] For example, you may think that your end of month targets will look bad. Label this. You have a ***thought*** that your end of month target is going to look bad. You may feel frustrated about this. Label this as a ***feeling*** of frustration. View your thoughts and feelings as transient data that may or may not be helpful to you.[152] This goes back to how we assign meaning to our stressors.

When you become mindful about your thoughts and your feelings, you can apply what you have learned about thought distortions. If I am having the thought that the end of month target will look bad, I can ask myself questions about it. How do I know that? What will happen if it is true? Will this truth cause me actual harm? What can I do about it? Who can help me? Use these moments of mindfulness to think more rationally and stop reacting emotionally out of habit.

We can use mindfulness to focus on things we enjoy too. Mindfulness should not focus exclusively on stressful times. We add to our own sense of well-being by noticing the things we find beautiful, peaceful, fun, exciting, adventurous, and joyful.

To begin to practice this on a daily basis, set a reminder on your phone to ask yourself the following:

- What is one thing I see today? What color is it?
- What is one thing I hear today? Is it loud or soft?
- What is one physical feeling I have right now? For example, you may feel your soft shirt or the keyboard beneath your fingertips.
- What is one thing I smell today? For example, can you smell coffee from the break room or an air freshener near your desk?
- What is one thing I taste today? For example, does your bottled water have added flavoring?
- What is one emotion I have today? For example, am I feeling content?

In reality, all we have is NOW. The minute that passed while reading the prior sentences is gone forever. You do not know what is in the next moment. Your moment is now. How aware are you right now about what is happening externally and internally?

For more practice with mindfulness, please visit the website www.revealedpotential.com to download your free workbook.

To increase our well-being, we need to retrain ourselves to think positively. All that has been mentioned so far certainly helps with that, but it would be incomplete without mentioning the benefits of practicing gratitude.

CHAPTER 9

Having an Attitude of Gratitude

Practicing gratitude daily has many benefits. We can literally change our lives by practicing gratitude. Gratitude takes us from a place of daily frustration to a place of well-being. Research backs this up too. Gratitude was found to provide these benefits:[153]

- Increases psychological well-being
- Lowers negative states like depression
- Reduces stress
- Increases social and emotional functioning
- Leads to better interpersonal relationships
- Makes us more giving/pro-social
- Improves sleep

I can attest to using the practice of gratitude to overcome stressful times. After my divorce, I went back to work full time with a school-aged child and all the housework and yardwork to maintain. Of course, after work I had to make dinner and help with homework. My weekends were spent grocery shopping, cleaning house, doing laundry, washing the car, and mowing the yard. I remember being sick and tired of feeling like I never had a day off. As I was halfway through mowing the yard one weekend, it hit me how any other single mom without a house and a yard for her kids would give her right arm to trade places with me. Wow! In a moment of weakness and self-pity, my brain kicked in with that grateful thought. I finished mowing the yard with a feeling of joy. I never minded mowing the yard again after that day.

Those who participated in a gratitude intervention by listing out what they felt grateful for each day reacted with less intensity to daily stressors.[154] It is easy to become overwhelmed with stress and let distorted thinking get a foothold in our minds. Gratitude helps to keep things in perspective.

Regular practice is also beneficial long term. In particular, having a generally grateful mood and feeling gratitude for others showed the strongest effects, with results lasting up to six months past the intervention.[155] This further supports the idea that gratitude improves well-being and interpersonal relationships. When we are grateful for others, we make more efforts in our relationships. When we take others for granted, we diminish those relationships.

When I developed burnout in my most recent job, I had lost a sense of gratitude. When I refocused myself, I could find things to be grateful about pretty easily. Sure, the job had its challenges and downsides, but all jobs do. Even people who own their own businesses talk about the downsides of their business. Simply working for someone else is not in and of itself a bad thing or less desirable than being your own boss. I had a salary that allowed me to live in the house I wanted, I had good health insurance, I worked with great people, and my hours were not bad. I could think of plenty of other jobs that would give me less return on my personal investment!

When we get stuck in assumptions and comparisons, we make ourselves very unhappy. At one point, I finally decided to apply for a new job. I was done and wanted out. I applied for a position three hours away, which involved relocating. It was in a coastal city that fit my long-term plans. I interviewed and was offered the job. I was so excited! It was a well-known company, and it was a newly created position. I had already started looking for new houses in that city prior to the job offer. However, the offer was not as exciting as I imagined it would be. Taking the position meant a slight pay cut, with a salary that capped out at less than what I could earn if I stayed where I was. The insurance was more expensive for less coverage. Then there was the loss of a company car. Despite assuming the position would be a fantastic change for me, when I evaluated the offer from a place of logic and not emotion, I chose to decline. The benefit of this experience was that it gave me a strong dose of gratitude once again. It felt good to know I was able to secure an offer at a company like that. At a point when I was back in that place of exhaustion, feeling cynical and believing I no longer made any kind of difference, my experience helped pull me out of the funk. Someone else did see my value. It helped to steer my mindset back to positive thinking.

When your current job falls short of helping you believe you add any value, search for that value yourself. You cannot wait for someone else to validate you. You may not be in a position to entertain job offers elsewhere for validation. Practicing gratitude about yourself is important too. Think of what you are grateful for in your experience, your education, how you have supported others, and the little ways you make a difference each day.

Gratitude is simple to practice. Simply list one good thing that happened each day. Or ask yourself: What three things am I truly grateful for today? What put a smile on my face? What beautiful thing did I notice? What words of inspiration did I hear?

A more advanced gratitude practice could be asking what lesson you learned from a particularly difficult or challenging situation. After my divorce, I spent time thinking about hard lessons I learned. Believe it or not, I made up my mind after learning about the affairs to be better and not bitter. When life lessons are boiled down, you either get better from the lessons learned or grow bitter with thoughts of failure and blame or feelings of hurt and anger. I knew that no matter how things ended up, I could not live my life with bitterness. I would be robbing myself of my joy in life.

To help kickstart your gratitude experience for your current job, consider the answers to these questions:

- What new skills have you learned on this job?
- Who has invested in you by way of support or guidance, even in a small way?
- What benefits have you received from this job?
- What has the salary from this job helped you to do?
- Who is considered a good friend at this job?
- How has this job stretched you or helped you to grow?
- During the hard times on this job, what lessons did you learn?

Sometimes we have to dig deep to come up with these answers. Many times, the small things we notice each day help us practice gratitude. The key here is to *practice* noticing the small things along with the big things. People who notice the small things and feel gratitude toward them tend to be happier. Rushing through life and never noticing the small things causes you to miss out on chances to build up your gratitude muscle.

Flexing your mindfulness and gratitude muscles are important for finding meaning in your work and life, which we will address in the next chapter. Have you noticed how many of the topics covered so far are intertwined with others? Challenging thought distortions can make it easier to have gratitude. When we are mindful and notice the details of our day, we can appreciate things we see and hear. We find meaning in our work when notice the value added to others when we support and mentor them. Recovery from burnout is a complex process, but making changes in one area often leads to transformation in other areas.

SECTION 4

Recovery For The Spirit

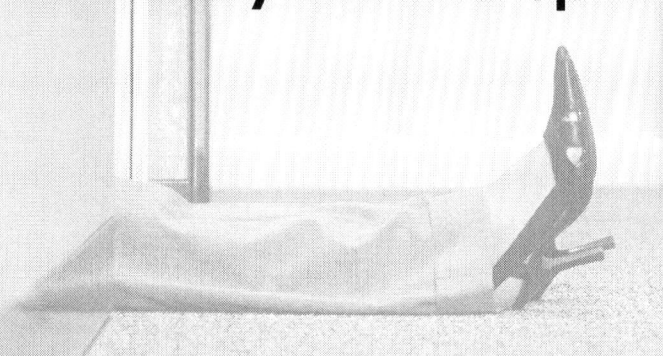

CHAPTER 10

Finding Meaning in Your Work

Unless born an heir or heiress, we all have to work. When we spend a significant portion of our waking hours on a job, we want it to be worthwhile. Those of us who are prone to burnout are not the type of people who are just there for a paycheck. If we were, chances are we would not have burned out. We experience burnout because we care a great deal about how our work makes a difference in our lives and those of others. Connection at work is critical too. As we have seen, isolation and lack of support both lead to burnout. We have higher ideals and get burned out when our efforts are influenced by organizational blocks, our perceptions, and our lack of self-care.

Meaning in life may be considered by answering these three questions:[156]

1. Where do I belong?
2. How do I connect and relate to others?
3. What is my value or my contribution to others?

As we saw during the pandemic, the great exodus from work shows just how relevant the topic of meaningful work is in our current environment. Back in 2017, this trend began among millennials. One article stated that millennials connecting their work to a higher purpose factored into their level of engagement and commitment to stay on the job.[157]

When we link our company's mission to something we personally believe and stand behind, we feel like we are serving a higher purpose. If we view our job as labor that only helps a corporation reach its profit margins, the work feels meaningless. Even when our tasks are routine, being aware of how those tasks contribute to a higher purpose fuels our sense of making a worthwhile contribution.

If you have pets, you may order food and toys from the company Chewy. I have been blown away by their superior customer service. Many customer service call centers or online chats provide negative experiences for the employee and the customer. Generally, I dread having to call a customer service line. I do not want to engage with people who seem to dislike their jobs and dislike you for bothering them. With Chewy, I have always had pleasant interactions. They instill a sense of purpose in their corporate culture. They love animals and know our furry friends are really family members. They demonstrate care in all customer service touchpoints. They even mail sympathy cards when you have lost your pet. The routine work in the call center is linked to a mission the employees support, and it makes a world of difference. Employees are part of a team that carries out that mission, giving them a sense of belonging. Their contribution with helping pet owners is an extension of one of their values—a love for animals.

Creating meaningfulness IN your work and AT your work requires thinking about the following:[158]

- **Role** — What am I doing?
- **Membership** — Where do I belong?
- **Identity** — Who am I?
- **Meaningfulness** — Why am I here?

Examples of answers to these questions come from two different angles. Some of you may be struggling to find any meaning at all with your current job.

From a Job Perspective:

- **Role** — My role is to procure parts in the service supply chain in the automotive industry.
- **Membership** — I belong to the After Service purchasing team.
- **Identity** — I am a leader of the procurement team, a coworker, a friend, and a resource to others in the supply chain.
- **Meaningfulness** — I procure the required parts to help car owners maintain the condition of their vehicles so that those vehicles serve the car owner's needs.

When I was actively experiencing burnout, I got stuck in the mindset that car parts do not make any difference in this world. This is an example of the cynicism and inefficacy of burnout. I became cynical about what was really an emergency order and what was just a game played by distributors to push everyone to meet their demands faster. My mindset was that their poor planning was always my emergency, and I was sick of it.

When I turned my mind back around, I focused on what I knew to be true emergencies. I thought about the family that needed that part for their car. I remembered a time when I was a single mom with one car. I was always concerned about possible issues that would leave me without a car. I had no backup transportation and would not be able to get my daughter to school or myself to work. The car parts did matter. Lack of a needed part impacted people on a very personal level.

If you are in a job where you are struggling to answer these questions, look at them from another point of view.

My personal reasons for doing this job:

- **Role** — I am working to obtain a paycheck to support my family. My role is to earn the funds for things we need.
- **Membership** — I belong to my children, my spouse, my church, my friendship group, and my community. I am also a member of my assigned group at work.
- **Identity** — I am a spouse, parent, community member who volunteers my time and donates money, and friend who helps when others are in need. I am a coworker who cares about others on my team.
- **Meaningfulness** — I am here to contribute to my children's future. I do this by creating a loving, stable, and secure home for my children so they can grow up to be all they can be. I contribute to the future of my community. My community is wherever I invest my time and energy and where I show care and commitment. My paycheck helps to support my ability to do this.

We need to feel a sense of belonging too. Connection is important to help us contend with daily stressors on the job. It can help us to know we are not alone when we have others to listen to our thoughts and feelings without fear of consequences.

Often our places of work fall short of promoting connection among employees. They tell a good story about teamwork but take actions to sabotage those connections. In this case, you can take the stance of a self-leader. We are all leaders in our own right and should own our role as a contributing member of the team. Even if not in a role titled as a leader, you can still initiate the following to help reduce the isolation you and others may be feeling.

Leaders can demonstrate caring by:[159]

- Encouraging trust and openness
- Demonstrating personalized attention
- Using humor
- Self-disclosure
- Displaying inclusiveness and compassion
- Understanding honest mistakes
- Providing support to others by expressing it and giving resources if possible
- Engaging in social rituals, like celebrating birthdays, attending appreciation dinners or holiday season get-togethers, and sending flowers for births and funerals

Please be aware that social get-togethers will flop if distrust exists on the team. They will seem superficial, and team members will want to escape the obligation as fast as they can. Again, these suggestions refer to typical work environments. Toxic work environments are rampant with distrust and self-protecting behaviors. I am not encouraging you to attempt to overcome a toxic work environment, though some of the strategies in this book may help you take better care of yourself while you work on your exit strategy.

In most circumstances, showing we care is usually reciprocated by others. You can get the ball rolling by implementing small but valuable behaviors to connect with others. One caveat I have to share, though, is to please be sincere as you work to foster connections.

For several years, I have observed employees doing all the "right" things without demonstrating a caring attitude. A coworker may walk by and ask how you are doing without slowing down to hear a response. He or she may say this to person after person while walking the aisles in the cube farm, never once stopping. Most would not even bother to reply. Take the time to make sure your actions match your words!

Job Crafting

One way to build more meaning into your work is through job crafting. This is where you actively review your job duties and add ways to use more of your values and skills. You initiate changes to the job demands and resources. Burnout happens when we do not find a good fit between our values, skill sets, and what the job requires us to do. Job crafting is about increasing our opportunities to build connections and our own competencies while effectively meeting job demands.

The dimensions suggested for job crafting are increasing structural job resources, social job resources, and challenging job demands.[160] Increasing structural job resources includes providing access to training and development or accessing existing job resources more effectively. Increasing social job resources refers to fostering collaboration and connection with others. Increasing challenging job demands may help with personal growth and avoiding the boredom that comes with routine demands.

Prior studies found that engagement is the opposite of burnout. Engagement entails vigor, dedication, and absorption.[161] Vigor is having energy, which we see as the opposite of the exhaustion in burnout. Dedication is still being committed and not cynical and detached. Absorption is being captivated to the point of not really noticing time going by rather than counting down the minutes until you can escape your cubicle. When you are absorbed because your efforts mean something, you find more intrinsic rewards in your work.

Have you ever worked on a project in your personal life that had you so engrossed you did not even notice the time? When we are being creative and doing work with personal meaning and personal rewards, we experience absorption.

Job crafting can help us find ways to instill a bit more vigor, dedication, and absorption in our work. Let me share some real-life examples of what I did to increase social and structural resources.

My team was often frustrated because we had key performance indicators (KPI) applied by our headquarters that could be sabotaged by others. We had zero control over the outcomes but were still judged by them. I could not change the KPI for our team at headquarters. Our headquarters were outside of the US, and that standard was applied globally for all the teams. The corporate cultural standard was simply too big to fight head on. Having no control over our work can lead to burnout.

Others had control over planning inventory and issuing purchase orders based on what they needed for restocking. My team was not consulted, and the capacity of the supplier was not taken into consideration. Often orders were issued for volumes the supplier could not fill in the timeframe allotted. This made them miss the target, which affected my team's score. The more often this happened, the lower the average score per month. When high volumes were put on order, suppliers could not adjust production to meet these demands, and our HQ would not allow more time than the standard, my team's score was out of our control.

As you can imagine, having your performance scores negatively affected by others and not having any voice can be frustrating. I had to find a way to alleviate some of this stress over something ultimately beyond my control.

To influence change, I collaborated with the team that planned inventory. In working to understand each other's challenges, we were able to discuss our supplier capacity issues and propose a purchasing plan that could increase the volume needed while giving the supplier a fighting chance to complete the orders. This became an area of expansion for our team. We crafted an area of our job where we could use skills of analysis, communication, and teamwork to influence higher levels of success. Instead of sitting back helpless and frustrated, we alleviated some of those feelings with job crafting. This falls into the category of increasing social job resources. While it did not solve every issue, it did provide some relief. It certainly reduced some resentment.

Think about an area of your job that is frustrating to you and write out what causes the frustration. If you can pinpoint the root issue, you might be able to craft a new way to deal with it. Consider what you value and what is at stake. How can you influence some change in this area? Who can help you? What resources could you access socially?

An example of increasing structural job resources would be to increase access to trainings to develop new skills. Not all companies offer development opportunities for their employees beyond the initial on-the-job training. They may allow their people to become stagnant in their growth. At one company where I worked, one of the main reasons given for leaving in exit interviews was the lack of training and development. Employees knew this equated to the lack of ability to get promoted.

If your job is not offering you development opportunities, you cannot sit back and hope someone else will do something about it. I have always been a big believer in investing in myself. I have not waited around for someone to value me enough to invest in me. I pursued additional trainings related to the supply chain to help collaborate with suppliers on possible solutions to problems they had filling our orders. Without this training, I may have been stuck trying the same old things that were not working. I would have lacked the additional knowledge I needed for advancement if I waited for my company to get me more training.

It will never be a waste of money to invest in yourself. Sure, the financial compensations may not be seen immediately, but growing personally and professionally are worthwhile endeavors. The return on the investment is often more than financial. When you invest in your own development, you increase your confidence, reduce your stress because you have additional tools in your toolbelt, and position yourself for future opportunities.

Think about the answers to these questions:

- What skills do I believe I need to learn to help with my daily work?
- What do I find difficult to do in my job?
- What do I wish I could do but rarely get the chance?

The third area of job crafting is increasing the challenge level. When I first started with one company after my divorce, I was bored out of my mind. I had skills and experience the company was not using. Out of boredom, I searched the computer system to learn more about the suppliers, parts, and customers. I explored areas above and beyond what was required of me because I was not being challenged in any way. I chose to make this effort to add value to myself and hopefully use it in the future. Eventually, when I changed teams and was then promoted, those efforts paid off.

Mentoring

An additional way to job craft is to become a mentor to another newer coworker or to accept a mentorship with someone you respect and admire in your company. This would be an example of increasing job challenges. Mentorship challenges you to learn new skills while increasing social job resources. Job challenge is not about making your job harder. It is about stretching yourself in order to grow. This may mean getting outside your comfort zone to do things your mentor suggests or by becoming a mentor yourself.

Four benefits result from being a mentor:[162]

- **Altruism** — Experiencing the joy of helping others
- **Cognition** — Gaining new skills or seeking out information to help others
- **Social Growth** — Developing a friendship as a result of the mentoring relationship
- **Personal Growth** — Developing self-confidence, pride, responsibility, and empathy

Values

It is important to create a list of what you value. If you are not able to articulate your values, you will have a harder time identifying which values fit with your current job. You may find that your current job helps you live out your values in your daily life. Conversely, if you find that very few values are in alignment with your current job, you may be better able to assess what you are looking for in a job as you develop an exit strategy. You do not want to jump into the next thing that comes along because it is different. Be sure opportunities align with your values, or you may be back in the same boat again.

To spark ideas, consider what is most important to you. Do you value honesty? Do you value serving others? Do you value creativity?

Others possible values include achievement, adventure, authenticity, balance, competence, fairness, health, humor, kindness, peace, recognition, respect, security, and wisdom. Make time to fully evaluate what you value and how those values are carried out in your everyday job situation and home life.

Additional values lists can be found on the internet if you want to learn more about them. You can also find a list in the workbook available to download for free from my website www.revealedpotential.com.

Finding meaning in our work can make going to work a more pleasant experience. For many of us in burnout, however, we allow the lack of joy in our job to transfer to a lack of joy in our life outside of work. Having joy outside of work can help in your recovery as well. We will examine ways to find time for enjoyable activities in the next chapter.

CHAPTER 11

Seek Joy on a Daily Basis

Finding meaningfulness in your work can lead to greater engagement, and that engagement can help lead to feelings of joy. However, your search for joy should extend to your daily life to help with your recovery. Work is not everything. We have many spheres in our lives, and work is just one part of the whole. This book is based on a holistic approach to recovery from burnout, addressing the mind, body, and spirit. At times when I sunk deeper and deeper into burnout, I drifted away from doing things I enjoyed. Most of my time was spent on things I "had" to do. Remember the mind distortions? Yes, I was using the one where I *have to do, should do, must do,* and so forth. Sure, we all have responsibilities, but I distorted things to the point I was no longer allowing time for relaxation and enjoyment. When I was out enjoying things, I felt guilty for all the things I was not getting done. I had it all wrong.

Curiosity

One way to experience joy is to welcome back that curious kid you used to be before you had to grow up and get serious about life. If you observe children, they are fascinated by so many things because those things are novel to them. As we grow up and experience more in life, we can become bored with things that are familiar. However, we need to strive to get some of that curiosity back if we want to experience joy.

Curiosity actually benefits us. Those with higher levels of curiosity tend to pursue and take advantage of varied opportunities, which makes for good days and ultimately a meaningful life.[163]

Enjoyment is comprised of the forward movement that comes from novelty and accomplishment.[164] When we watch children learning new things each day, they are deeply engaged by the novelty and squeal with delight when they have something figured out. As time goes on, the relationship between growth and enjoyment tends to wane.[165] Often our time at school told us what to think and not how to think. It took the curiosity out of the learning, which then dampened the level of enjoyment. As adults we can curate our own experience of learning new things. We do not have to sit in a classroom while someone tells us what to think. We can go out and discover a whole world of novel ideas and experiences.

Earlier I mentioned the concept of absorption, where time flies because we are deeply engaged in what we are doing. Absorption is central to curiosity.[166] This is what I wanted when I used to sigh and think to myself that I was dying a slow death in my cubicle each day. I was not using my skills or values. The work was routine, without any feedback or mention of how it mattered to anyone. When I began to get curious, I accessed the computer system to learn more about the parts, suppliers, and customers. That curiosity got me through the time until I changed teams and learned new skills.

Curiosity benefits us in a variety of ways:

- It leads to absorption and vigor, mentioned earlier as being the opposites of burnout
- It helps us to accept the challenges we face more easily
- It encourages us to be open to new experiences and ideas
- It leads to a generally more positive outlook
- It increases our endurance to pursue answers and solve issues

Have you ever met a person who was absolutely alive with enthusiasm? Many wish people like that would just chill out! But why should they? In reality we should strive to be more like them. They are the ones who are curious about life, open to new experiences, and not worried about failing because trying is so much fun.

In a work setting, curiosity was studied based on four dimensions. The researchers titled and described the four dimensions as such:[167]

- **Joyous Exploration** — Seeking opportunities to expand skills and working through complex problems
- **Deprivation Sensitivity** — Working tirelessly to find answers to complex questions; not able to rest until finding a solution
- **Stress Tolerance** — Exploring instead of avoiding when work causes anxiety; distress doesn't lower the motivation to take on new projects; does not shy away from the unknown or unfamiliar
- **Openness to People's Ideas** — Feeling it is important to listen to ideas from people who think differently

US workers who scored higher in joyous exploration had a correlation to the dimensions of engagement (vigor, dedication, and absorption) and job crafting.[168] Engagement is on the opposite end of the continuum from burnout. I knew curiosity helped me get excited about life again, but I stopped using it, which led me deeper into burnout.

I employed the value of curiosity when I was rebuilding my life after divorce. At first, I was anxious about what my new future held for me until it dawned on me that I got a do-over. Once I started seeing my life as an exciting do-over adventure, the anxiety diminished. I felt excited about the possibilities.

Finally I realized that reframing could help me recover from burnout. I felt like my spark had left me. I missed the excitement I had felt a few short years earlier.

When I decided to get curious about the problems I faced at work rather than getting annoyed or avoiding them, I engaged other skill sets. If we are bored, getting curious leads to creativity. Even though I did not understand the value of what I was doing at the time, I am grateful something sparked new ideas rather than continuing to die a slow death in my cubicle.

The study on the four dimensions of curiosity also stated that stress tolerance and openness to people's ideas were strongly linked to workplace well-being.[169] Begin to be curious about the things causing anxiety at work instead of avoiding them. Connect with more people so you can hear their ideas, which are different from your own. You can increase your social support resources by doing this.

Get Your Bucket List Started

I realize some may not like the term "bucket list," as it refers to what to do before you die. Many people die long before their hearts stop beating. They are the working dead who move through their days enduring each hour until they go home and start all over again the next day. Call your list whatever you want, but embrace the idea of dreaming about new experiences. So many of us have listened to messages throughout life that say dreaming is a waste of time. It isn't. How do you think innovative ideas come about? The dreamers give the world innovative ideas. The key to growth is taking action to make those dreams come true.

Many people dream and never take action. After a while, others see their dreaming as a waste of time. Some dreams are solely fantasy. I will never be a good singer because I was not gifted with the vocal cords to produce any kind of sound others would want to hear. I do not waste my time dreaming I will be the lead singer of a rock band.

The kinds of dreams that change your life are more about what is possible. There are more possibilities for you than may you realize. Once you are willing to dream about what is possible, begin to take steps toward making it happen. Keep adding to your list as new and interesting things catch your attention.

My bucket list includes things big and small. One of my bigger bucket list items was to write a book. I took action, and this book is the result! Previously I made a goal to run a 5K. I did that and moved on to running half marathons. Now I foster excitement for my half marathons by choosing different locations to run them. I have travel sites I want to see; I want to hike the El Camino across Spain. These goals also include growth opportunities. Some of my certifications were on my bucket list. I am happiest when I am growing as a person and experiencing new things in life. I grow discontent when I become stagnant.

Here are some areas that can help jumpstart your list. Get a notebook and promise yourself you will begin to fill this in, add to it, and take action to fulfill your dreams!

- Places to see
- Books to read
- Experiences to have
- Growth/Learning
- Foods to try
- Concerts, plays, comedy clubs
- Friend time
- Family time

Hopefully these categories can help get the ball rolling for some ideas. Your list can be anything you want it to be, organized however you want it to be. The important thing is taking action one step at a time.

Create Margin

In order to have time for self-care and to create joy in your life, you have to be intentional about how you spend your time. Creating margin means building time in your schedule to allow you to complete necessary tasks while still having hours left in the day or week to do what you really want to do.

Many of us live for the weekends or to get to our next vacation without enjoying all the days in between them. That is not a life of joy. That is a life of endurance. I have seen many memes online and on inspirational sites that tell us if we create the kind of life we love, we will not need a vacation from it. This is all about creating meaning and joy in our day-to-day lives. We create pockets of time to take care of ourselves, spend time with family and friends, and reduce the stress of work demands. It is about giving each day a higher quality of life.

Vacations are great, and I believe in planning ahead to make sure you actually take them. I do not believe that you will never need a vacation once you create a life you enjoy. We all need small moments and big moments to have variety. Do not allow yourself to become stuck in a life of endurance, waiting to get some relief on the weekends or when you do finally get a vacation. Seek out a joyful experience at least once every day. At the end of your day, think about what you enjoyed about it. This keeps the positive thoughts and feelings in your conscious awareness and helps to create those neural pathways.

While living a busy life, and especially while experiencing burnout, you may wonder how you will find margin in your day. You may be losing time in ways you may not have realized and wondering why you never get to what you really want to do, but there are techniques to help you create margin.

The 80/20 Rule

One of the best protectors of how we spend time is to apply the 80/20 rule. This means that 20% of the items on your to-do list create about 80% of the impact. So often we fill up our to-do list at work or at home and begin to check off all the small things first. It is a psychological reward to check things off and feel like you are making progress. However, you may find that you get to the end of your day and still have big requirements looming over your head that require working past normal hours.

The next time you make a list of things to do, look at what all the tasks will give you in return. Does answering emails the first hour of your day get that the report done that is due by 5:00 p.m.? I have learned that working on important tasks for sixty-ninety minutes will get things moving along nicely. Then I take a break. You may take a walk, listen to phone messages, or answer emails. However, those emails and phone messages do not take priority. Park them on your list until you have worked through higher priority items first, such as returning to your project or moving to the next most important item of the day.

When some of your daily tasks involve deliverables to people on other teams or your supervisor, ask for a deadline. That will help you assess how urgent the task is. Some things are important but not urgent. You can prioritize based on this information.

What Is Important and Urgent?

You may be wondering how you determine what falls into the 20% and what is important enough to do first, second, or third.

In the book *The 7 Habits of Highly Effective People*, Stephen R. Covey introduced the matrix of important, urgent, not important, and not urgent. This book is a classic, and I strongly recommend you find a copy if you have not read it yet. If you have read it, you may want to revisit it and apply what he teaches.

- Tasks that meet the criteria of **important and urgent** are crisis situations or projects that have deadlines.
- Tasks that meet the criteria of **important but not urgent** are things like connecting with other team members, looking for new opportunities to add meaning in your work, or tasks that are for the prevention of possible issues.
- Tasks that are **not important, but urgent (to other people)** are meetings, interruptions to ask you for information, some emails, and phone calls.
- Tasks that are **not important and not urgent** are essentially the time wasters. This is busy work that serves no higher purpose, some phone calls and emails, and time wasters such as scrolling through social media or binge-watching something on television.[170]

Some highly driven people may categorize play time and self-care under not urgent and not important, but with some thoughtfulness, we can plan our burnout recovery with this tool. You can get a handle on your day and use it to create margin. The not urgent and not important should not keep you at the office past your scheduled time. This tool can help you see things for what they really are. In burnout we tend to place more importance on things than they truly warrant.

By not filling up your day with so many tasks, you can plan that walk in the park after work or meeting your friend for a dinner that you have been putting off forever.

If you work in a place that has a lot going on around you, it may be challenging at first to discern what is important and urgent when others make everything sound urgent. I have experienced this in several places I have worked. Boundary setting is of great value when assessing our priorities.

Boundaries

Setting boundaries with ourselves and others is critical to our recovery. You may be surprised I mention setting a boundary with yourself. I learned the hard way that I needed to understand my own limits before I could stop letting others take advantage of me and taking on more than I could handle.

Capacity and Delegation

It is important to evaluate your capacity to add more to your plate and whether a task requires you to be the one to do it. Other people will use up your time if you allow them. Some people will go so far as to place their responsibilities on you. When others are in charge of your time and your tasks, do you think you will have the margin in your life to do what it is you really want to do?

Evaluate requests of your time asking these questions:

1. Can I effectively take this on? (Does it fit my schedule? Can I complete it the way it needs to be completed without undue levels of stress? What value is there in doing this?)
2. Can someone else do it? (Is there someone else who can effectively take this on instead of me? Why does it have to be me? Who else has the knowledge and skills to do this? Is there a reason I will not delegate this task to someone else?)

3. Why can this person not do it for themselves? (Is there a real need for them to ask for help? Can they complete part of this request themselves? Is this a task they are avoiding by dumping it on me?)

The Power of No

You need to get comfortable with the word **no**. You can learn polite ways to turn down requests.

Simple ways to say no politely include:

- That project sounds really interesting, but right now I cannot devote the proper time and attention to it.
- I am sorry things are a challenge for you right now. I wish I could help, but I am unable at this time.
- I am concerned about not being able to meet the deadline on this request with everything else I have going on. I think it is best for me to decline.
- I appreciate you thinking of me, but the timing is not good for me right now.

Notice that I did not qualify my responses. Part of setting a boundary is to set it without having to justify why you set it. If the other person insists that you qualify your boundary, then that person does not respect boundaries. A person who respects boundaries will simply reply back that they understand.

You do not owe others any explanation for saying no. Saying no is your right. It is not your problem if they have issues with this. How they choose to react is their issue.

You may think there is no way on earth you can tell your boss no. That is often true. If this is a work situation, talk with your supervisor about the requests made and your concerns. Any leader worth their salt will listen to your concerns and help you find a way to either make the request fit or help find other resources.

If your boss is not a good leader, still present information to him or her. Ask if you can split the task with someone else if you think it is too big for you to take on alone. If you must be the sole person to work on this task, share ideas about other work tasks that may be pushed out while you prioritize this one. The key here is to communicate. Do not accept your fate and become stressed out without any resources.

The way you communicate with your boss is important. Supervisors want to hear that you will complete your tasks and give them what they need when they need it. Let your boss know that you want to provide that support and need their help prioritizing tasks. This allows you to have some sense of control over your work tasks and reduce stress.

Get a Handle on Codependency

I have to be vigilant about codependency. For years, I felt I had to be responsible for far more outcomes than were mine to own. I felt a responsibility FOR people and worked hard to control outcomes. Now I understand I have a responsibility TO people, which allows them to take ownership of what is theirs to handle. I do my part, but I do not take on everyone else's part too.

If you constantly feel that you have to take care of things for others and fear the outcomes if they do not do what they should be doing, then you have a codependency issue. It is nothing to be ashamed of. Many of us struggle with this and were given messages as children that fueled this thought distortion. We may have been blamed for the way others felt. Maybe you were told to make sure another relative was protected from reality by constantly working to control the outcomes of situations so they did not have to be responsible. Do not teach others learned helplessness. If you do, you will forever be worn out by their demands.

This is a heavy burden to carry psychologically and gives us the illusion of having control. You do not have control of what others do. You never did. Sometimes things appeared as though you had control, but often that was just dumb luck. You only have as much control as others will let you have. The more you try to control everything, the more you spiral out of control. Look at all the extra duties you take on that are not yours. Look at the time and energy expended to attempt to stay ahead of it all. Think about the stress you have added to your daily life doing this. There is no payoff for any of this.

Not accepting help from others is another aspect of codependency. We try to please others and avoid being a burden to anyone. We then try to tackle more than we should when we really need help, and we add to our stress. If you refuse to give up the need for control and delegate, this aspect of codependency rears its ugly head. You exacerbate the exhaustion in burnout, along with the cynicism. After a while you begin to resent all the burdens you have taken on while others seem to have it easy.

If you are struggling with codependency, I encourage you to learn more about it and possibly seek counseling with someone who can help you recognize patterns that need to be broken. If left unaddressed, it will sabotage your burnout recovery. Those so busy taking on everyone else's responsibilities will never have time for themselves.

The last facet of developing a meaningful life and a life of joy involves spirituality. I am not talking about religion, but who you are in connection to your world beyond your work. You are not your work title. You are so much more than that!

CHAPTER 12

Feeding Your Spirit

What is spirituality exactly? So often the word seems to be dogmatic and confusing. Some fear that others will impose beliefs on them that they do not have. Spirituality is individual to each person.

Spirituality often involves a belief in a higher power or higher universal laws. Across world religions, that higher power may be God, Jesus, or Allah. For some it is simply a belief in a creator who is universal and the giver of life. For others it may be nature itself.

I appreciate the definition Search Institute uses to help define spiritual development: "Authentically expressing one's strengths, identity, passions, values, and creativity through relationships, activities, and/or practices that shape bonds with oneself, family, community, humanity, the world, and/or that which one believes to be transcendent or sacred."[171]

Spirituality refers to your connection to some kind of higher power, other people, and what you believe brings peace to your inner being. The word I want to emphasize is connection. When we are in burnout, we often feel disconnected and untethered. We can feel like we are trudging along day by day without a sense of purpose. We feel that there has to be more to life than what we are doing.

Spirituality is vital to your recovery from burnout. Feeling alone and adrift in the world is a disconnection to Spirit. I use the word Spirit capitalized to refer to that higher being or higher consciousness; I refer to your inner spirit with lower case. We must make time for connection with Spirit. Spend time with others who believe as you do. Being in community with others can help you deepen your relationship with Spirit and feed your inner spirit. Those who regularly feel "blessed, connected and transcendent" are less likely to have the exhaustion associated with burnout.[172] That feeling of being blessed links directly back to gratitude.

Many of the topics covered in this book help to feed our spirits. Meditation and mindfulness are forms of looking inward to gain a sense of peace. Healthier thinking helps us to recover from burnout, while distorted thinking can destroy our peace! Curiosity taps into creativity and imagination. Our conscience results from the values and beliefs we have that either lead us to feel good or bad about what we do or feel. If we live and work in alignment with our values and beliefs, we feel as though we have a sense of purpose. The daily practice of spirituality, regardless of the exact religious or spiritual belief, reduces the likelihood of the characteristics of burnout.[173]

The one important area we have not addressed is love. Love is the basis for all of this. We must love others if we are to have connection and purpose. We must love ourselves enough to walk this journey of burnout recovery. We have love for our higher power or creator when we act in accordance with what we perceive as our creator's will for our lives.

In the excellent book *Called Out—Why I Traded Two Dream Jobs for a Life of True Calling,* Paula Faris describes her relentless drive for success in her career and her belief that God would not have put that on her heart if it was not her true calling. However, as she discovered, your vocation and your true faith calling may not be the same. She shares that God can show you how to carry out your true faith calling within your vocation, regardless of what that vocation may be.[174]

Death By Cubicle

Often, we push ourselves to the breaking point, believing that what we are doing is what we were called to do. We think if we do not succeed in that particular profession, we will not be carrying that out. What we fail to understand is that it may be packaged in a different way. I can carry out my true faith calling in a variety of careers. Our true faith calling is the living out of our values and gifts. We have flexibility in how those are applied. Your calling is who you have been created to be, not what you do for a living.[175]

Transcending the limited view that our purpose is found in our career can be life changing. I am created to be so much more than what I get paid to do. Finding purpose and meaning in my work certainly helps, but this is about growing beyond that limited view. For many world religions and spiritual beliefs, it comes down to love. When we love our creator and others in the world, we fulfill that connection we need and gain a sense of belonging. We find our calling in this life is to love others. We do this in our everyday life when we share a kind word, help another who cannot help themselves, pray or send positive thoughts for the benefit of others, and live in harmony. We carry out our faith calling when we act in accordance with making the world a better place. We can make a difference where we are in the moment with small acts of love. Our world distorts what is considered successful. It usually presents success as someone making a certain income, having a certain title, or gaining a certain number of followers on social media. Success for your life is what YOU define it to be. The world will ask you to be over committed and under connected.

I am a Christian and have found the Bible to be a great source of strength in trying times. The wisdom contained within reminds me I am not alone. I have a loving creator who has great plans for me, plans to help me prosper and never to harm me. The wisdom comes from Spirit and connects me to Spirit when I read and study those words. You may not believe as I do, and I respect that. I do hope you find ways to connect to your higher power and come to know you have a calling beyond your career. I hope you find ways to hear that inner voice to discern between choices that are helpful or those that could be harmful to you. A branch not connected to the vine cannot bear fruit. It is simply just a twig.

Some helpful ways to practice spirituality include spending quiet time in nature, listening to inner hunches, and paying attention to what others are telling you, especially if you have heard the same message from several people. Learn to be still and quiet all the inner chatter. Silence the radio, TV, and social media videos as well. If we stay distracted with being busy all the time and have constant chatter from internal or external sources, connecting with our higher source is more challenging.

Journaling your thoughts, feelings, hunches, and what you notice when you mindful are all ways to develop a deeper connection with yourself and Spirit. The more you journal, the more likely you will be to recognize a unifying theme guiding who you are called to be. You might also study books that speak to your beliefs with other like-minded people. You can share with each other what stood out to you as you read. Insights from others may be a source of inspiration for you.

Try not to complicate spirituality. Simply love yourself, love others, and learn to be still so you can connect with your higher power. Silence the distractions for an established period of time on a consistent basis. You choose the schedule. The key here is to be consistent.

CONCLUSION

Well, my friend, we have covered a lot of territory together on this journey to recovery. There is not any one magic bullet for curing burnout. Many complex processes affect our jobs, our heads, our hearts, and our bodies. It takes a variety of strategies to build a recovery plan that is effective. As you think about your values and how well your current job aligns with them, you may find you have more misses than hits. If that is the case, you now have the opportunity to craft an exit strategy. Avoid acting from a reactionary state and think about what you are really looking for in a job the next time around.

If you have not taken the time to journal through this process or download the workbook, I encourage you to do that. You can find the workbook at www.revealedpotential.com.

What symptoms of burnout did you recognize in yourself? Think about the symptoms of exhaustion, feeling cynical, and not believing you are doing anything effective or meaningful. Spend some time writing about each of those areas to identify what stands out the most.

Of these symptoms, which do you believe is having the most negative impact on you? After referring back to the chapter that addresses this symptom, what strategies can you implement for yourself to begin to improve this issue?

You have already taken the first big step in your recovery by reading this book. Based on your journal notes just now, you can choose your next step. Do not worry about a right way or wrong way to do this. I believe all these areas are intertwined, and as we add each piece, we get further and further along in our recovery. Just start with what speaks to you first. You know yourself and what you are going through. I do hope that as time goes on, you will see the value of adding in all the pieces and how they work together to bring about wellness.

Wellness is the goal here. It is not about finding the perfect job to never experience burnout again. That job does not exist. This is about building up our resiliency to prevent burnout. It is about the stress management we need to practice daily. It is about challenging the thinking distortions that fuel our perceptions of what is stressful and what is not. It is about the care we take to get the kinds of nutrients we need to reduce oxidative stress and neurodegeneration. It is about lifting that fog and thinking more clearly.

Not every day will be the model of burnout recovery. No one is perfect, and crazy days happen. That is okay. Being mindful on those days will help. Make a commitment to yourself to get a good night's sleep, pack that healthy lunch the next day, or go for a walk after work. If you fall off the horse, get back in the saddle. Do not let too many days go by that lack wellness actions. If you let too many days go by without incorporating what you have learned, you are at risk for relapse. Trust me on this. I began to backslide even as I was writing this book. It is very easy to let it happen. Fortunately, I corrected my course and am being mindful of my choices each day once again.

Wellness is a way of life. Recovery from burnout requires maintenance. It does not happen on autopilot. If you are back on autopilot, you may be experiencing the frog in hot water metaphor. Only you can take charge of your wellness. No one can make the commitment and do the work on your behalf. You decide how the next chapter of your life will be written because you are its author. Your decisions now determine what is written. I encourage you to implement the strategies I shared from my journey to recovery. I also invite you to stay connected by joining the Facebook group Death by Cubicle. Check the website www.revealedpotential.com to stay up to date about opportunities for additional learning, coaching, and retreats. Be well, my friend!

ENDNOTES

1. Gallup Research Team, "Gallup's Perspective on Employee Burnout: Causes and Cures," Gallup, January 24, 2020, https://www.gallup.com/workplace/282668/employee-burnout-perspective-paper.aspx.
2. Ewa Gruszczynska, Beata A. Basinska, and Wilmar B. Schaufeli, "Within- and Between-Person Factor Structure of the Oldenburg Burnout Inventory: Analysis of a Diary Study Using Multilevel Confirmatory Factor Analysis," ed. Karl Bang Christensen, *PLOS ONE* 16, no. 5 (May 14, 2021): e0251257, https://doi.org/10.1371/journal.pone.0251257.
3. Christina Maslach, Wilmar B. Schaufeli, and Michael P. Leiter, "Job Burnout," *Annual Review of Psychology* 52 (2001): 398.
4. Maslach, Schaufeli and Leiter, "Job Burnout," 400.
5. Maslach, Schaufeli and Leiter, "Job Burnout," 401.
6. "Maslach Burnout Toolkit for General Use - Mind Garden," Mind Garden, accessed January 15, 2022, https://www.mindgarden.com/332-maslach-burnout-toolkit-for-general-use.
7. "Free Stress Test: Assess Your Burnout and Job Stress," Test-Stress, n.d., https://www.test-stress.com/en/free-burnout-test.php.
8. Maslach, Schaufeli and Leiter, "Job Burnout," 403.
9. Wilmar B. Schaufeli and Arnold B. Baker, "Job Demands, Job Resources, and Their Relationship with Burnout and Engagement: A Multi-Sample Study," *Journal of Organizational Behavior* 25, no. 3 (May 2004): 307.
10. Wilmar B. Schaufeli and Arnold B. Baker, "Job Demands," 294.
11. Evangelia Demerouti et al., "The Job Demands-Resources Model of Burnout," *Journal of Applied Psychology* 86, no. 3 (2001): 501, https://doi.org/10.1037/0021-9010.86.3.501.
12. Maslach, Schaufeli and Leiter, "Job Burnout," 414-415.
13. Maslach, Schaufeli and Leiter, "Job Burnout," 414.
14. Yunsoo Lee and SunHee J. Eissenstat, "A Longitudinal Examination of the Causes and Effects of Burnout Based on the Job Demands-Resources Model," *Int J Educ* 18 (June 8, 2018): 341, https://doi.org/https://doi.org/10.1007/s10775-018-9364-7.
15. Maslach, Schaufeli and Leiter, "Job Burnout," 414.

[16] Yunsoo Lee and SunHee J. Eissentstat, "A Longitudinal Examination of the Causes," 341.
[17] Maslach, Schaufeli and Leiter, "Job Burnout," 414.
[18] Maslach, Schaufeli and Leiter, "Job Burnout," 415.
[19] Mujdelen Yener and Ozgun Coskun, "Using Job Resources and Job Demands in Predicting Burnout," *Procedia-Social and Behavioral Sciences* 99 (2013): 871, 875, https://doi.org/doi:10.1016/j.sbspro.2013.10.559.
[20] Maslach, Schaufeli and Leiter, "Job Burnout," 415.
[21] Mujdelen Yener and Ozgun Coskun, "Using Job Resources and Job Demands in Predicting Burnout," 871, 875.
[22] Maslach, Schaufeli and Leiter, "Job Burnout," 415.
[23] Christina Surawicz, "J. Edward Berk Distinguished Lecture: Avoiding Burnout," *The American Journal of Gastroenterology* 109 (April 2014): 512.
[24] Yunsoo Lee and SunHee J. Eissentstat, "A Longitudinal Examination of the Causes," 348.
[25] Christina Maslach and Susan E. Jackson, "The Role of Sex and Family Variables in Burnout," *Sex Roles* 12, no. 7/8 (1985): 848; Siw Tone Innstrand et al., "Exploring Within- and Between-Gender Differences in Burnout: 8 Different Occupational Groups," *Int Arch Occup Environ Health* 84 (2011): 821, https://doi.org/DOI 10.1007/s00420-011-0667-y.
[26] Siw Tone Innstrand et al., "Exploring Within- and Between-Gender Differences in Burnout," 821.
[27] Christina Maslach and Susan E. Jackson, "The Role of Sex and Family Variables in Burnout," 848.
[28] Christina Maslach and Susan E. Jackson, "The Role of Sex and Family Variables in Burnout," 848.
[29] Christina Maslach and Susan E. Jackson, "The Role of Sex and Family Variables in Burnout," 848.
[30] Arnold B. Bakker et al., "The Relationship Between the Big Five Personality Factors and Burnout: A Study Among Volunteer Counselors," *The Journal of Social Psychology* 146, no. 1 (2006): 34-38.
[31] Arnold B. Bakker et al., "The Relationship between the Big Five Personality Factors," 34.
[32] Arnold B. Bakker et al., "The Relationship between the Big Five Personality Factors," 37.
[33] Arnold B. Bakker et al., "The Relationship between the Big Five Personality Factors," 43.

[34] Niall Bolger, "Coping as a Personality Process: A Prospective Study," *Journal of Personality and Social Psychology* 59, no. 3 (1990): 533.

[35] Arnold B. Bakker et al., "The Relationship between the Big Five Personality Factors," 45.

[36] Howard Mertz, "Stress and the Gut," n.d., 1, https://www.med.unc.edu/ibs/wp-content/uploads/sites/450/2017/10/Stress-and-the-Gut.pdf.

[37] L. Michael Romero and Luke K. Butler, "Endocrinology of Stress," *International Journal of Comparative Psychology* 20, no. 2 (2007): 89–95, https://escholarship.org/uc/item/87d2k2xz.

[38] Oliva Evans-Guy, "Amygdala Function and Location," Simply Psychology, May 9, 2021, https://simplypsychology.org/amygdala.html, 1.

[39] Kara E. Hannibal and Mark D. Bishop, "Chronic Stress, Cortisol Dysfunction, and Pain: A Psychoneuroendocrine Rationale for Stress Management in Pain Rehabilitation," *Journal of American Physical Therapy Association* 94, no. 12 (July 14, 2014): 1818, https://doi.org/10.2522/ptj.201305097.

[40] L. Michael Romero and Luke K. Butler, "Endocrinology of Stress," 90.

[41] Kara E. Hannibal and Mark D. Bishop, "Chronic Stress, Cortisol Dysfunction, and Pain," 1818.

[42] L. Michael Romero and Luke K. Butler, "Endocrinology of Stress," 90.

[43] Howard Mertz, "Stress and the Gut," 2.

[44] Tanja C. Adam and Elissa S. Epel, "Stress, Eating and the Reward System," *Physiology & Behavior* 91 (2007): 450, https://www.academia.edu/25314585/Stress_eating_and_the_reward_system.

[45] Howard Mertz, "Stress and the Gut," 2.

[46] Tanja C. Adam and Elissa S. Epel, "Stress, Eating and the Reward System," 452.

[47] F. Cavagnini et al., "Glucocorticoids and Neuroendocrine Function," *International Journal of Obesity* 24, no. Suppl 2 (2000): S77.

[48] Tanja C. Adam and Elissa S. Epel, "Stress, Eating and the Reward System," 454-455.

[49] Laura E. Finch and A. Janet Tomiyama, "Stress-Induced Eating Dampens Physiological and Behavioral Stress Responses," in *Nutrition in the Prevention and Treatment of Abdominal Obesity*, (2019), 190, https://doi.org/10.1016/B978-0-12-816093-0.00015-X.

[50] Tanja C. Adam and Elissa S. Epel, "Stress, Eating and the Reward System," 455.

[51] Janet M. Torpy, "Chronic Stress and the Heart," ed. Richard M. Glass, JAMA Patient Page, October 10, 2007, www.jama.org.

52. Jaskanwal D. Sara et al., "Association Between Work-Related Stress and Coronary Heart Disease: A Review of Prospective Studies Through Job Strain, Effort-Reward Balance, and Organizational Justice Models," *J Am Heart Assoc* 7 (2018): 9, https://doi.org/10.1161/JAHA.117.008073.
53. Jaskanawal D. Sara et al., "Association between Work-Related Stress and Coronary Heart Disease," 8.
54. Jaskanawal D. Sara et al., "Association between Work-Related Stress and Coronary Heart Disease," 8.
55. Howard Mertz, "Stress and the Gut," 1.
56. Howard Merz, "Stress and the Gut," 3.
57. Laura Dumitrescu et al., "Oxidative Stress and the Microbiota-Gut-Brain Axis," *Oxidative Medicine and Cellular Longevity* 2018 (December 9, 2018): 5, https://doi.org/10.1155/2018/2406594.
58. Shruti Shandilya et al., "Interplay of Gut Microbiota and Oxidative Stress: Perspective on Neurodegeneration and Neuroprotection," *Journal of Advanced Research*, (2021): 11, https://doi.org/10.1016/j.jare.2021.09.005.
59. Laura Dumitrescu et al., "Oxidative Stress and the Microbiota-Gut-Brain Axis," 7.
60. Kara E. Hannibal and Mark D. Bishop, "Chronic Stress, Cortisol Dysfunction, and Pain," 1820.
61. Steve Chaney, "Which Muscles Are Affected by Stress," Chaney Health, August 18, 2020, https://chaneyhealth.com/healthtips/which-muscles-are-affected-by-stress/.
62. Kara E. Hannibal and Mark D. Bishop, "Chronic Stress, Cortisol Dysfunction, and Pain," 1819.
63. P. Lehrer, "Anger, Stress, Dysregulation Produces Wear and Tear on the Lung," *Thorax* 6, no. 10 (2006): 833, https://doi.org/10.1136/thx.2006.057182.
64. Paul Forsythe et al., "Opposing Effects of Short- and Long-Term Stress on Airway Inflammation," *American Journal of Respiratory and Critical Care Medicine* 169 (2004): 224, https://doi.org/10.1164/rccm.200307-979OC.
65. P. Lehrer, "Anger, Stress, Dysregulation Produces Wear and Tear on the Lung," 833.
66. Suzanne C. Segerstrom and Gregory E. Miller, "Psychological Stress and the Human Immune System: A Meta-Analytic Study of 30 Years of Inquiry," *Psychol Bull.* 130, no. 4 (February 7, 2006): 617, https://www.ncbi.nlm.nih.gov/pmc/articles/PMC1361287/.

[67] US Department of Health and Human Services, "Understanding the Immune System-How It Works," NIH Publication 03-5423 (September 2003), http://www.imgt.org/IMGTeducation/Tutorials/ImmuneSystem/UK/the_immune_system.pdf, 7.

[68] US Department of Heath and Human Services, "Understanding the Immune System-How It Works," 8.

[69] US Department of Heath and Human Services, "Understanding the Immune System-How It Works," 16.

[70] Airin Martinez, Lillian Ruelas, and Douglas Granger, "Household Fear of Deportation in Relation to Chronic Stress and Salivary Proinflammatory Cytokines in Mexican-Origin Families Post-SB 1070," *SSM-Population Health* 5 (2018): 197-198, https://doi.org/10.1016/j.ssmph.2018.06.003.

[71] Petra C. Arck et al., "Neuroimmunology of Stress: Skin Takes Center Stage," *Journal of Investigative Dermatology* 126, no. 8 (2006): 1697, https://doi.org/10.1038/sj.jid.5700104.

[72] Petra C. Arck et al., "Neuroimmunology of Stress: Skin Takes Center Stage," 1703.

[73] Soorih Shaikh et al., "Prevalence of Hair Loss and Stress as the Cause; a Cross-Sectional Study," *International Journal of Advanced Research* 4, no. 7 (July 2016): 332, https://doi.org/10.2147/IJAR01.

[74] Kendra Cherry, "5 Surprising Way That Stress Affects Your Brain," ed. Carly Snyder, MD, Very Well Mind, April 8, 2021, https://www.verywellmind.com/surprising-ways-that-stress-affects-your-brain-2795040.

[75] Sangya Singh and Aditi Vats, "Impact of Physiological and Psychological Stress on Students," *The Pharma Innovation Journal* 9, no. 4 (2020): 113.

[76] University of California - Berkeley, "How Chronic Stress Predisposes Brain to Mental Disorders," Science Daily, February 11, 2014, https://www.sciencedaily.com/releases/2014/02/140211153559.htm.

[77] M.Y.L. Oei et al., "Psychosocial Stress Impairs Working Memory at High Loads: An Association with Cortisol Levels and Memory Retrieval," *Stress* 9, no. 3 (September 2006): 139, https://doi.org/10.1080/10253890600965773.

[78] Charlotte Madore et al., "Microglia, Lifestyle Stress, and Neurodegeneration," *Immunity* 52, no. 2 (February 18, 2020): 224, https://doi.org/10.1016/j.immuni.2019.12.003.

[79] Sami Ouanes and Julius Popp, "High Cortisol and the Risk of Dementia and Alzheimer's Disease: A Review of the Literature," *Frontiers in*

Aging Neuroscience 11 (March 1, 2019): 8, https://doi.org/10.3389/fnagi.2019.00043.

[80] Sami Ouanes and Julius Popp, "High Cortisol and the Risk of Dementia and Alzheimer's Disease," 1.

[81] Arnaud Metlaine et al., "Sleep and Biological Parameters in Professional Burnout: A Psychophysiological Characterization," *PloS ONE* 13, no. 1 (2018): 6, https://doi.org/10.1371/journal.pone.0190607.

[82] Arnaud Metlaine et al., "Sleep and Biological Parameters in Professional Burnout," 7.

[83] Arnaud Metlaine et al., "Sleep and Biological Parameters in Professional Burnout," 8.

[84] Arnaud Metlaine et al., "Sleep and Biological Parameters in Professional Burnout," 15.

[85] Gundry MD Team, "10 Vitamin D Deficiency Symptoms You Can Identify," Gundry MD, February 19, 2018, https://gundrymd.com/vitamin-d-deficiency-symptoms/.

[86] R. Liu et al., "Association between Sleep Quality and C-Reactive Protein: Results from National Health and Nutrition Examination Survey, 2005-2008," *PLoS ONE* 9, no. 3 (March 24, 2014): 10, https://doi.org/10.1371/journal.pone.0092607.

[87] Dorit Koren, Katie L. O'Sullivan, and Babak Mokhlesi, "Metabolic and Glycemic Sequelae of Sleep Disturbances in Children and Adults," *Curr Diab Rep* 15, no. 562 (November 14, 2014): 5, https://doi.org/10.1007/s11892-014-0562-5.

[88] C.F. Siengsukon and L.A. Boyd, "Does Sleep Promote Motor Learning? Implications for Physical Rehabilitation," *Physical Therapy* 89, no. 4 (2009): 374.

[89] L. Exelmans and J. Van den Bulck, "Bedtime Mobile Phone Use and Sleep in Adults," *Social Science and Medicine* 148 (2016): 12, https://doi.org/10.1016/j.socscimed.2015.11.037.

[90] L. Exelmans and J. Van den Bulck, "Bedtime Mobile Phone Use and Sleep in Adults," 11.

[91] T. J. Xu and A.C. Reichelt, "Sucrose or Sucrose and Caffeine Differentially Impact Memory and Anxiety-like Behaviours, and Alter Hippocampal Parvalbumin and Doublecortin," *Neuropharmacology* 137 (July 2018): 26, https://doi.org/https://doi.org/10.1016/j.neuropharm.2018.04.012.

[92] Feng Ding et al., "How Is Satiety Affected When Consuming Food While Working on a Computer," *Nutrients* 11, no. 1545 (July 8, 2019): 12, https://doi.org/10.3390/nu11071545.

[93] Ronan Doherty et al., "Sleep and Nutrition Interactions: Implications for Athletes," Nutrients 11, no. 822 (2019): 1, https://doi.org/10.3390/nu11104822.

[94] Molly E. Zimmerman et al., "Neuropsychological Function Response to Nocturnal Blue Light Blockage in Individuals with Symptoms of Insomnia: A Pilot Randomized Controlled Study," *Journal of the International Neuropsychological Society* 25 (2019): 668, https://doi.org/10.1017/S1355617719000055.

[95] Molly E. Zimmerman et al., "Neuropsychological Function Response to Nocturnal Blue Light Blockage in Individuals with Symptoms of Insomnia," 674.

[96] P. Ramchandani and et al., "A Systematic Review of Treatments for Settling Problems and Night Waking in Young Children," ed. June Thompson, *Community Practitioner* 73, no. 3 (March 2000): 528.

[97] Mayo Clinic Staff, "Sleep Tips: 6 Steps to Better Sleep," Mayo Clinic, April 17, 2020, https://www.mayoclinic.org/healthy-lifestyle/adult-health/in-depth/sleep/art-20048379.

[98] Mayo Clinic Staff, "Sleep Tips: 6 Steps to Better Sleep."

[99] Xiao Meng et al., "Dietary Sources and Bioactivities of Melatonin," *Nutrients* 9, no. 367 (April 17, 2017): 43, https://doi.org/10.3390/nu9040367.

[100] Xiao Meng et al., "Dietary Sources and Bioactivities of Melatonin," 43.

[101] Ronan Doherty et al., "Sleep and Nutrition Interactions: Implications for Athletes," 8.

[102] Hayk S. Arakelyan, *Drinks to Help You Sleep* (2021), 1, https://www.academia.edu/44816596/Drinks_to_Help_You_Sleep.

[103] Hayk S. Arakelyan, *Drinks to Help You Sleep*, 1.

[104] Hsiao-Han Lin et al., "Effect of Kiwifruit Consumption on Sleep Quality in Adults with Sleep Problems," *Asia Pac J Clin Nutr* 20, no. 2 (2011): 169.

[105] K.V. Jesperson et al., "Music for Insomnia in Adults," *Cochrane Database Syst Rev* 8 (August 13, 2015): 2, https://doi.org/10.1002/14651858.CD010459.pub2.

[106] A.S. Keyhanmehr et al., "The Effect of Aromatherapy with Rosa Damascena Essential Oil on Sleep Quality in Children," *Research Journal of Pharmacognosy* 51, no. 1 (December 27, 2017): 41.

[107] Z Najafi, Tagharrobi Z, and Shahriyari-Kale-Masihi M, "Effect of Aromatherapy with Lavender on Sleep Quality among Patients Undergoing Hemodialysis," *Feyz* 18, no. 2 (2014): 145.

[108] William N. Setzer, "Essential Oils and Anxiolytic Aromatherapy," *Natural Product Communications* 4, no. 9 (2009): 1305–10.

[109] Ravindra P. Nagendra, Nirmala Maruthai, and Bindu M. Kutty, "Meditation and Its Regulatory Role on Sleep," *Frontiers in Neurology* 3, no. 54 (April 18, 2012): 2, https://doi.org/10.3389/fneur.2012.00054.

[110] Jim Kwik, "Discover 10 Powerful Hacks to Unlock Your Superbrain to Learn Faster, Comprehend More and Forget Less," Mindvalley, 2022, https://www.mindvalley.com/superbrain/masterclass?itm_source=google_free_courses_L2leftbanner&itm_campaign=evergreen_sb&_ga=2.199694828.335883068.1642872239-778299405.1642872239.

[111] Shibu M. Poulose, Amanda N. Carey, and Barbara Shukitt-Hale, "Improving Brain Signaling in Aging: Could Berries Be the Answer?" *Expert Reviews* 12, no. 8 (2012): 887, https://doi.org/10.1586/ERN.12.86.

[112] Barbara Shukitt-Hale, "Blueberries and Neuronal Aging," *Gerontology* 2012, no. 58 (August 16, 2012): 520, https://doi.org/10.1159/000341101.

[113] Robert Krikorian et al., "Blueberry Supplementation Improves Memory in Older Adults," *J Agric Food Chem* 58, no. 7 (April 14, 2010): 4000, https://doi.org/10.1021/jf9029332.

[114] Shih Jen Tan and Intan Safinar Ismail, "Potency of Selected Berries, Grapes, and Citrus Fruit as Neuroprotective Agents," *Evidence-Based Complementary and Alternative Medicine* 2020 (May 30, 2020): 4, https://doi.org/10.1155/2020/3582947.

[115] Robert Krikorian et al., "Concord Grape Juice Supplementation Improves Memory Function in Older Adults with Mild Cognitive Impairment," *British Journal of Nutrition* 103 (December 23, 2009): 732, https://doi.org/10.1017/S0007114509992364.

[116] Astrid C.J. Nooyens et al., "Fruit and Vegetable Intake and Cognitive Decline in Middle-Aged Men and Women: The Doetinchem Cohort Study," *British Journal of Nutrition* 106 (2011): 757, https://doi.org/10.1017/S0007114511001024.

[117] Peter Pribis et al., "Effects of Walnut Consumption on Cognitive Performance in Young Adults," *British Journal of Nutrition* 107 (2012): 1398, https://doi.org/10.1017/S0007114511004302.

[118] Emma Derbyshire, "Brain Health across the Lifespan: A Systematic Review on the Role of Omega-3 Fatty Acid Supplements," *Nutrients* 10, no. 1094 (2018): 12-13, https://doi.org/10.3390/nu10081094.

[119] Freydis Hjalmarsdottir, MS, "12 Foods That Are Very High in Omega-3," Healthline, September 30, 2019, https://www.healthline.com/nutrition/12-omega-3-rich-foods.

[120] Astrid Nehlig, "Effects of Coffee/Caffeine on Brain Health and Disease: What Should I Tell My Patients?" *Pract Neurol* 16 (2016): 94, https://doi.org/10.1136/practneurol-2015-001162.

[121] Tarah Venn, "Food Fix: Best Foods to Fight Fatigue," Healthline Channel, YouTube video, 2:11, 2020, https://www.youtube.com/watch?v=DDQHFN61nU8&t=7s&ab_channel=Healthline.

[122] David C. Nieman et al., "Bananas as an Energy Source during Exercise: A Metabolomics Approach," *PLoS ONE* 7, no. 5 (May 2012): e37479, https://doi.org/10.1371/journal.pone.0037479.

[123] Andrea M. Weinstein and Kirk I. Erickson, "Healthy Body Equals Healthy Mind," *Journal of the American Society on Aging* 35, no. 2 (2011): 96.

[124] Andrea M. Weinstein and Kirk I. Erickson, "Healthy Body Equals Healthy Mind," 96.

[125] Nada Sallam and Ismail Laher, "Exercise Modulates Oxidative Stress and Inflammation in Aging and Cardiovascular Diseases," *Oxidative Medicine and Cellular Longevity* 2016, no. 7239639 (2016): 3-4, https://doi.org/10.1155/2016/7239636.

[126] Yan Yang et al., "Sedentary Behavior and Sleep Problems: A Systematic Review and Meta-Analysis," *Int. J. Behav.Med.* 24 (2017): 488, https://doi.org/10.1007/s12529-016-9609-0.

[127] J. Fanning et al., "Replacing Sedentary Time with Sleep, Light, or Moderate-To-Vigorous Physical Activity: Effects on Self-Regulation and Executive Functioning," *J Behav Med* 40 (2017): 338, https://doi.org/10.1007/s10865-016-9788-9.

[128] Linda Larkey et al., "Meditative Movement as a Category of Exercise: Implications for Research," *Journal of Physical Activity and Health* 6 (2009): 233.

[129] Denise Rizzolo et al., "Stress Management Strategies for Students: The Immediate Effects of Yoga, Humor and Reading on Stress," *Journal of College Teaching and Learning* 6, no. 8 (2009): 85.

[130] Geoffrey W. Melville et al., "Fifteen Minutes of Chair-Based Yoga Postures or Guided Meditation Performed in the Office Can Elicit a Relaxation Response," *Evidence-Based Complementary and Alternative Medicine* (2012): 8, https://doi.org/10.1155/2012/501986.

[131] Nate Klemp, "The Neuroscience of Breaking out of Negative Thinking (and How to Do It in under 30 Seconds) Your Brain Is Wired to Focus on the Negative. Here's How to Build a New, More Positive, Mindset Anytime, Anywhere," Inc., August 7, 2019, https://www.inc.com/

nate-klemp/try-this-neuroscience-based-technique-to-shift-your-mindset-from-negative-to-positive-in-30-seconds.html.
132. Nate Klemp, "The Neuroscience of Breaking out of Negative Thinking," 1.
133. Rick Hanson, *Your Wonderful Brain* (2007), 5, https://s3-us-west-1.amazonaws.com/fwb-media.rickhanson.net/PDFfiles/YourWonderfulBrain.pdf.
134. Rick Hanson, *Your Wonderful Brain*, 5.
135. Rick Hanson, *Your Wonderful Brain*, 8.
136. Rick Hanson, *Your Wonderful Brain*, 8.
137. Rick Hanson, *Your Wonderful Brain*, 8.
138. Rick Hanson, *Your Wonderful Brain*, 7.
139. Martin E.P. Seligman, *Flourish* (2011; repr., New York, NY: Atria Paperback, 2013), 189.
140. John Kabat-Zinn, *Wherever You Go, There You Are* (New York: Hyperion, 1994), 4.
141. Rachel M. Abenavoli et al., "The Protective Effects of Mindfulness against Burnout among Educators," *The Psychology of Education Review* 37, no. 2 (2013): 66.
142. Rachel M. Abenavoli et al., "The Protective Effects of Mindfulness against Burnout among Educators," 66.
143. Arunas Antanaitis, "Mindfulness in the Workplace Benefits and Strategies to Integrate Mindfulness-Based Programs in the Workplace," *Oohna Journal* Fall/Winter (2015): 39.
144. Arunas Antanaitis, "Mindfulness in the Workplace Benefits and Strategies to Integrate Mindfulness-Based Programs in the Workplace," 40.
145. Kirk Warren Brown and Richard M. Ryan, "The Benefits of Being Present: Mindfulness and Its Role in Psychological Well-Being," *Journal of Personality and Social Psychology* 84, no. 4 (2003): 823, https://doi.org/10.1037/0022-3514.84.4.822.
146. Shauna L. Shapiro et al., "Mechanisms of Mindfulness," *Journal of Clinical Psychology* (2006): 3, https://doi.org/10.1002/jclp.20237.
147. Shauna L. Shapiro et al., "Mechanisms of Mindfulness," 8.
148. Shauna L. Shapiro et al., "Mechanisms of Mindfulness," 8.
149. Shauna L. Shapiro et al., "Mechanisms of Mindfulness," 8.
150. Shauna L. Shapiro et al., "Mechanisms of Mindfulness," 9.
151. Susan David and Christina Congleton, "Emotional Agility," in *The HBR Emotional Intelligence Series-Mindfulness* (Boston: Harvard Business Review Press, 2017), 65.

[152] Susan David and Christina Congleton, "Emotional Agility,"65.
[153] Courtney E. Ackerman, "28 Benefits of Gratitude & Most Significant Research Findings," Positive Psychology, December 14, 2021, https://positivepsychology.com/benefits-gratitude-research-questions/.
[154] Izabela Krejtz et al., "Counting One's Blessings Can Reduce the Impact of Daily Stress," *J Happiness Stud* 2016, no. 17 (September 30, 2014): 35, https://doi.org/10.1007/s10902-014-9578-4.
[155] Ernst T. Bohlmeijer et al., "Promoting Gratitude as a Resource for Sustainable Mental Health: Results of a 3-Armed Randomized Controlled Trial up to 6 Months Follow-Up," *Journal of Happiness Studies* 2021, no. 22 (May 7, 2020): 1026, https://doi.org/10.1007/s10902-020-00261-5.
[156] Susan Cartwright and Nicola Holmes, "The Meaning of Work: The Challenge of Regaining Employee Engagement and Reducing Cynicism," *Human Resources Management Review* 16 (2006): 202, https://doi.org/10.1016/j.hrmr.2006.03.012.
[157] Candace Moody, "Change Your Life by Finding Your Purpose on the Job," *Florida Times Union*, December 13, 2017.
[158] Michael G. Pratt and Blake E. Ashforth, "Fostering Meaningfulness in Work and at Work," in *Positive Organizational Scholarship: Foundations of a New Discipline*, ed. K.S. Cameron, J.E. Dutton, and R. E. Quinn (San Francisco: Berrett-Koehler, 2003), 312.
[159] Michael G. Pratt and Blake E. Ashforth, "Fostering Meaningfulness in Work and at Work," 318.
[160] Cristina-Ioana Dan, Andra Catalina Rosca, and Alexandru Mateizer, "Job Crafting and Performance in Firefighters: The Role of Work Meaning and Work Engagement," *Frontiers in Psychology* 11, no. 894 (May 20, 2020): 8, https://doi.org/10.3389/fpsyg.2020.00894.
[161] Cristina-Ioana Dan, Andra Catalina Rosca, and Alexandru Mateizer, "Job Crafting and Performance in Firefighters," 3.
[162] Susan Beltman and Marcel Schaeben, "Institution-Wide Peer Mentoring: Benefits for Mentors," *The International Journal of the First Year in Higher Education* 3, no. 2 (August 2012): 41, https://doi.org/10.5204/intjfyhe.v3i2.124.
[163] Todd B. Kashdan, Paul Rose, and Frank D. Fincham, "Curiosity and Exploration: Facilitating Positive Subjective Experiences and Personal Growth Opportunities," *Journal of Personality Assessment* 82, no. 3 (2004): 292.
[164] Mihaly Csikszentmihalyi, Flow (New York: Harper Perennial, 1990), 46.

[165] Mihaly Csikszentmihalyi, Flow (New York: Harper Perennial, 1990), 47.
[166] Todd B. Kashdan, Paul Rose, and Frank D. Fincham, "Curiosity and Exploration," 292.
[167] Todd B. Kashdan et al., "Curiosity Has Comprehensive Benefits in the Workplace: Developing and Validating a Multidimensional Workplace Curiosity Scale in United States and German Employees," *Personality and Individual Differences* 155 (2020): 7, https://doi.org/10.1016/j.paid.2019.109717.
[168] Todd B. Kashdan et al., "Curiosity Has Comprehensive Benefits in the Workplace," 10.
[169] Todd B. Kashdan et al., "Curiosity Has Comprehensive Benefits in the Workplace," 11.
[170] Stephen R. Covey, *The Seven Habits of Highly Effective People* (New York: Fireside-Simon & Schuster, 1989), 151.
[171] Search Institute Staff, "What Is Spiritual Development?" Search Institute, 2021, https://www.search-institute.org/our-research/youth-development-research/spiritual-development/.
[172] Jason M. Holland and Robert A. Neimeyer, "Reducing the Risk of Burnout in End-of-Life Care Settings: The Role of Daily Spiritual Experiences and Training," *Palliative and Supportive Care* 3 (November 7, 2005): 178, https://doi.org/10.1017/S1478951505050297.
[173] Jason M. Holland and Robert A. Neimeyer, "Reducing the Risk of Burnout in End-of-Life Care Settings," 178.
[174] Paula Faris, *Called Out* (Bloomington, MN: Bethany House Publishers, 2020), 123.
[175] Paula Faris, *Called Out*, 123.

BIBLIOGRAPHY

Abenavoli, Rachel M., Patricia A. Jennings, Mark T. Greenburg, and Deirdre A. Katz. "The Protective Effects of Mindfulness against Burnout among Educators." *The Psychology of Education Review* 37, no. 2 (2013): 57–69.

Ackerman, Courtney E. "28 Benefits of Gratitude & Most Significant Research Findings." Positive Psychology. December 14, 2021. https://positivepsychology.com/benefits-gratitude-research-questions/.

Adam, Tanja C., and Elissa S. Epel. "Stress, Eating and the Reward System." *Physiology & Behavior* 91 (2007): 449–58. https://www.academia.edu/25314585/Stress_eating_and_the_reward_system.

Anacker, Christoph, Patricia A. Zunszain, Livia A. Carvalho, and Carmine M. Pariente. "The Glucocorticoid Receptor: Pivot of Depression and of Antidepressant Treatment?" *Psychoneuroendocrinology* 36 (2011): 415–25. https://doi.org/10.1016/j.psyneun.2010.03.007.

Antanaitis, Arunas. "Mindfulness in the Workplace Benefits and Strategies to Integrate Mindfulness-Based Programs in the Workplace." *Oohna Journal* Fall/Winter 2015 (2015): 39–42.

Arakelyan, Hayk S. *Drinks to Help You Sleep.* 2021. https://www.academia.edu/44816596/Drinks_to_Help_You_Sleep.

Arck, Petra C., Andrzej Slominski, Theoharis C. Theoharides, Eva M. Peters, and Ralf Paus. "Neuroimmunology of Stress: Skin Takes Center Stage." *Journal of Investigative Dermatology* 126, no. 8 (2006): 1697–1704. https://doi.org/10.1038/sj.jid.5700104.

Bakker, Arnold B., Karen I. Van Der Zee, Kerry A. Lewig, and Maureen F. Dollard. "The Relationship Between the Big Five Personality Factors and Burnout: A Study Among Volunteer Counselors." *The Journal of Social Psychology* 146, no. 1 (2006): 31–50.

Beltman, Susan, and Marcel Schaeben. "Institution-Wide Peer Mentoring: Benefits for Mentors." *The International Journal of the First Year in Higher Education* 3, no. 2 (August 2012): 33–44. https://doi.org/10.5204/intjfyhe.v3i2.124.

Bohlmeijer, Ernst T., Jannis T. Kraiss, Philip Watkins, and Marijke Schotanus-Dijkstra. "Promoting Gratitude as a Resource for Sustainable Mental Health: Results of a 3-Armed Randomized Controlled Trial up to 6 Months Follow-Up." *Journal of Happiness Studies* 2021, no. 22 (May 7, 2020): 1011–32. https://doi.org/10.1007/s10902-020-00261-5.

Bolger, Niall. "Coping as a Personality Process: A Prospective Study." *Journal of Personality and Social Psychology* 59, no. 3 (1990): 525–37.

Brown, Kirk Warren, and Richard M. Ryan. "The Benefits of Being Present: Mindfulness and Its Role in Psychological Well-Being." *Journal of Personality and Social Psychology* 84, no. 4 (2003): 822–48. https://doi.org/10.1037/0022-3514.84.4.822.

Cartwright, Susan, and Nicola Holmes. "The Meaning of Work: The Challenge of Regaining Employee Engagement and Reducing Cynicism." *Human Resources Management Review* 16 (2006): 199–208. https://doi.org/10.1016/j.hrmr.2006.03.012.

Cavagnini, F., M. Croci, M.L. Petroni, and C. Invitti. "Glucocorticoids and Neuroendocrine Function." *International Journal of Obesity* 24, no. Suppl 2 (2000): S77–79.

Chaney, Steve. "Which Muscles Are Affected by Stress." Chaney Health. August 18, 2020. https://chaneyhealth.com/healthtips/which-muscles-are-affected-by-stress/.

Cherry, Kendra. "5 Surprising Way That Stress Affects Your Brain." Edited by Carly Snyder, MD. Very Well Mind. April 8, 2021. https://www.verywellmind.com/surprising-ways-that-stress-affects-your-brain-2795040.

Covey, Stephen R. *The Seven Habits of Highly Effective People.* New York: Fireside-Simon & Schuster, 1989.

Csikszentmihalyi, Mihaly. *Flow.* New York: Harper Perennial, 1990.

Dan, Cristina-Ioana, Andra Catalina Rosca, and Alexandru Mateizer. "Job Crafting and Performance in Firefighters: The Role of Work

Meaning and Work Engagement." *Frontiers in Psychology* 11, no. 894 (May 20, 2020). https://doi.org/10.3389/fpsyg.2020.00894.

David, Susan, and Christina Congleton. "Emotional Agility." In *The HBR Emotional Intelligence Series-Mindfulness*, 55–70. Boston: Harvard Business Review Press, 2017.

Demerouti, Evangelia, Arnold B. Bakker, Friedhelm Nachreiner, and Wilmar B. Schaufeli. "The Job Demands-Resources Model of Burnout." *Journal of Applied Psychology* 86, no. 3 (2001): 499–512. https://doi.org/10.1037/0021-9010.86.3.499.

Derbyshire, Emma. "Brain Health Across the Lifespan: A Systematic Review on the Role of Omega-3 Fatty Acid Supplements." *Nutrients* 10, no. 1094 (2018). https://doi.org/10.3390/nu10081094.

Ding, Feng, Nazimah Hamid, Daniel Shepherd, and Kevin Kantono. "How Is Satiety Affected When Consuming Food While Working on a Computer." *Nutrients* 11, no. 1545 (July 8, 2019). https://doi.org/10.3390/nu11071545.

Doherty, Ronan, Sharon Madigan, Giles Warrington, and Jason Ellis. "Sleep and Nutrition Interactions: Implications for Athletes." *Nutrients* 11, no. 822 (2019). https://doi.org/10.3390/nu1104822.

Dumitrescu, Laura, Iulia Popescu-Olaru, Liviu Cozma, Delia Tulba, Mihail Eugen Hinescu, Laura Cristina Ceafalan, Mihaela Gherghiceanu, and Bodgan Ovidiu Popescu. "Oxidative Stress and the Microbiota-Gut-Brain Axis." *Oxidative Medicine and Cellular Longevity* 2018 (December 9, 2018): 1–12. https://doi.org/doi.org/10.1155/2018/2406594.

Evans-Guy, Oliva. "Amygdala Function and Location." Simply Psychology. May 9, 2021. https://simplypsychology.org/amygdala.html.

Exelmans, L., and J. Van den Bulck. "Bedtime Mobile Phone Use and Sleep in Adults." *Social Science and Medicine* 148 (2016): 1–25. https://doi.org/10.1016/j.socscimed.2015.11.037.

Fanning, J., G. Porter, E. A. Awick, D.K. Ehlers, S. A. Roberts, G. Cooke, A. Z. Burzynska, M. W. Voss, A. F. Kramer, and E. McAuley. "Replacing Sedentary Time with Sleep, Light, or Moderate-To-Vigorous Physical Activity: Effects on Self-Regulation and

Executive Functioning." *J Behav Med* 40 (2017): 332–42. https://doi.org/10.1007/s10865-016-9788-9.

Faris, Paula. *Called Out*. Bloomington, MN: Bethany House Publishers, 2020.

Finch, Laura E., and A. Janet Tomiyama. "Stress-Induced Eating Dampens Physiological and Behavioral Stress Responses." *Nutrition in the Prevention and Treatment of Abdominal Obesity* (2019): 189–95. https://doi.org/10.1016/B978-0-12-816093-0.00015-X.

Forsythe, Paul, Cory Ebeling, John R. Gordon, A. Dean Befus, and Harissios Vliagoftis. "Opposing Effects of Short- and Long-Term Stress on Airway Inflammation." *American Journal of Respiratory and Critical Care Medicine* 169 (2004): 220–26. https://doi.org/10.1164/rccm.200307-979OC.

"Free Stress Test: Assess Your Burnout and Job Stress." Test-Stress. https://www.test-stress.com/en/free-burnout-test.php.

Gallup Research Team. "Gallup's Perspective on Employee Burnout: Causes and Cures." Gallup. January 24, 2020. https://www.gallup.com/workplace/282668/employee-burnout-perspective-paper.aspx.

Gruszczynska, Ewa, Beata A. Basinska, and Wilmar B. Schaufeli. "Within- and Between-Person Factor Structure of the Oldenburg Burnout Inventory: Analysis of a Diary Study Using Multilevel Confirmatory Factor Analysis." Edited by Karl Bang Christensen. *PLOS ONE* 16, no. 5 (May 14, 2021): e0251257. https://doi.org/10.1371/journal.pone.0251257.

Gundry MD Team. "10 Vitamin D Deficiency Symptoms You Can Identify." Gundry MD. February 19, 2018. https://gundrymd.com/vitamin-d-deficiency-symptoms/.

Hannibal, Kara E., and Mark D. Bishop. "Chronic Stress, Cortisol Dysfunction, and Pain: A Psychoneuroendocrine Rationale for Stress Management in Pain Rehabilitation." *Journal of American Physical Therapy Association* 94, no. 12 (July 14, 2014): 1816–25. https://doi.org/10.2522/ptj.201305097.

Hanson, Rick. "Your Wonderful Brain." Wisebrain. 2007. https://s3-us-west-1.amazonaws.com/fwb-media.rickhanson.net/PDFfiles/YourWonderfulBrain.pdf.

Hjalmarsdottir, MS, Freydis. "12 Foods That Are Very High in Omega-3." Healthline. September 30, 2019. https://www.healthline.com/nutrition/12-omega-3-rich-foods.

Holland, Jason M., and Robert A. Neimeyer. "Reducing the Risk of Burnout in End-of-Life Care Settings: The Role of Daily Spiritual Experiences and Training." *Palliative and Supportive Care* 3 (November 7, 2005): 173–81. https://doi.org/10.1017/S1478951505050297.

Innstrand, Siw Tone, Ellen Melbye Langballe, Erik Falkum, and Olaf Gjerlow Aasland. "Exploring Within- and Between-Gender Differences in Burnout: 8 Different Occupational Groups." *Int Arch Occup Environ Health* 84 (2011): 813–24. https://doi.org/10.1007/s00420-011-0667-y.

Jesperson, K.V., J. Koenig, P. Jennum, and P. Vuust. "Music for Insomnia in Adults." *Cochrane Database Syst Rev* 8 (August 13, 2015). https://doi.org/10.1002/14651858.CD010459.pub2.

Kabat-Zinn, John. *Wherever You Go, There You Are*. New York: Hyperion, 1994.

Kashdan, Todd B., Fallon R. Goodman, David J. Disabato, Patrick E. McKnight, Kerry Kelso, and Carl Naughton. "Curiosity Has Comprehensive Benefits in the Workplace: Developing and Validating a Multidimensional Workplace Curiosity Scale in United States and German Employees." *Personality and Individual Differences* 155 (2020). https://doi.org/10.1016/j.paid.2019.109717.

Kashdan, Todd B., Paul Rose, and Frank D. Fincham. "Curiosity and Exploration: Facilitating Positive Subjective Experiences and Personal Growth Opportunities." *Journal of Personality Assessment* 82, no. 3 (2004): 291–305.

Keyhanmehr, A.S., M. Movahhed, S. Sahranavard, L. Gachkar, M. Hamish, Sh. Afsharpaiman, and H. Nikfarjad. "The Effect of Aromatherapy with Rosa Damascena Essential Oil on Sleep Quality in Children." *Research Journal of Pharmacognosy* 51, no. 1 (December 27, 2017): 41–46.

Klemp, Nate. "The Neuroscience of Breaking out of Negative Thinking (and How to Do It in under 30 Seconds) Your Brain

Is Wired to Focus on the Negative. Here's How to Build a New, More Positive, Mindset Anytime, Anywhere." Inc. August 7, 2019. https://www.inc.com/nate-klemp/try-this-neuroscience-based-technique-to-shift-your-mindset-from-negative-to-positive-in-30-seconds.html.

Koch, Jennifer. "Balancing Spirituality and Work." Workforce. September 1, 1995. https://workforce.com/news/balancing-spirituality-and-work.

Koren, Dorit, Katie L. O'Sullivan, and Babak Mokhlesi. "Metabolic and Glycemic Sequelae of Sleep Disturbances in Children and Adults." *Curr Diab Rep* 15, no. 562 (November 14, 2014). https://doi.org/10.1007/s11892-014-0562-5.

Krejtz, Izabela, John B. Nezlek, Anna Michnicka, Paweł Holas, and Marzena Rusanowska. "Counting One's Blessings Can Reduce the Impact of Daily Stress." *J Happiness Stud* 2016, no. 17 (September 30, 2014): 25–39. https://doi.org/10.1007/s10902-014-9578-4.

Krikorian, Robert, Tiffany A. Nash, Marcelle D. Shidler, Barbara Shukitt-Hale, and James A. Joseph. "Concord Grape Juice Supplementation Improves Memory Function in Older Adults with Mild Cognitive Impairment." *British Journal of Nutrition* 103 (December 23, 2009): 730–34. https://doi.org/10.1017/S0007114509992364.

Krikorian, Robert, Marcelle D. Shidler, Tiffany A. Nash, Wilhelmina Kalt, Melinda R. Vinqvist-Tymchuk, Barbara Shu Kitt-Hale, and James A. Joseph. "Blueberry Supplementation Improves Memory in Older Adults." *J Agric Food Chem* 58, no. 7 (April 14, 2010): 3996–4000. https://doi.org/10.1021/jf9029332.

Kwik, Jim. "Discover 10 Powerful Hacks to Unlock Your Superbrain to Learn Faster, Comprehend More and Forget Less." Mindvalley. 2022. https://www.mindvalley.com/superbrain/masterclass?itm_source=google_free_courses_L2leftbanner&itm_campaign=evergreen_sb&_ga=2.199694828.335883068.1642872239-778299405.1642872239.

Larkey, Linda, Roger Jahnke, Jennifer Etnier, and Julie Gonzalez. "Meditative Movement as a Category of Exercise: Implications for Research." *Journal of Physical Activity and Health* 6 (2009): 230–38.

Lee, Yunsoo, and SunHee J. Eissenstat. "A Longitudinal Examination of the Causes and Effects of Burnout Based on the Job

Demands-Resources Model." *Int J Educ* 18 (June 8, 2018): 337–54. https://doi.org/10.1007/s10775-018-9364-7.

Lehrer, P. "Anger, Stress, Dysregulation Produces Wear and Tear on the Lung." *Thorax* 6, no. 10 (2006): 833–34. https://doi.org/10.1136/thx.2006.057182.

Lin, Hsiao-Han, Pei-Shan Tsai, Su-Chen Fang, and Jen-Fang Lui. "Effect of Kiwifruit Consumption on Sleep Quality in Adults with Sleep Problems." *Asia Pac J Clin Nutr* 20, no. 2 (2011): 169–74.

Liu, R., X. Liu, P.C. Zee, L. Hou, Z. Zheng, Y. Wei, and J. Du. "Association between Sleep Quality and C-Reactive Protein: Results from National Health and Nutrition Examination Survey, 2005-2008." *PLoS ONE* 9, no. 3 (March 24, 2014). https://doi.org/10.1371/journal.pone.0092607.

Madore, Charlotte, Zhuoran Yin, Jeffrey Leibowitz, and Oleg Butovsky. "Microglia, Lifestyle Stress, and Neurodegeneration." *Immunity* 52, no. 2 (February 18, 2020): 222–40. https://doi.org/10.1016/j.immuni.2019.12.003.

Martinez, Airin, Lillian Ruelas, and Douglas Granger. "Household Fear of Deportation in Relation to Chronic Stress and Salivary Proinflammatory Cytokines in Mexican-Origin Families Post-SB 1070." *SSM-Population Health* 5 (2018): 188–200. https://doi.org/10.1016/j.ssmph.2018.06.003.

"Maslach Burnout Toolkit for General Use - Mind Garden." Mind Garden, Accessed January 15, 2022. https://www.mindgarden.com/332-maslach-burnout-toolkit-for-general-use.

Maslach, Christina, and Susan E. Jackson. "The Role of Sex and Family Variables in Burnout." *Sex Roles* 12, no. 7/8 (1985): 837–51.

Maslach, Christina, Wilmar B. Schaufeli, and Michael P. Leiter. "Job Burnout." *Annual Review of Psychology* 52 (2001): 397–422.

Mayo Clinic Staff. "Sleep Tips: 6 Steps to Better Sleep." Mayo Clinic. April 17, 2020. https://www.mayoclinic.org/healthy-lifestyle/adult-health/in-depth/sleep/art-20048379.

McCrae, Robert R., and Paul T. Costa. "Personality, Coping, and Coping Effectiveness in an Adult Sample." *Journal of Personality* 54, no. 2 (June 1986): 385–405.

Melville, Geoffrey W., Dennis Chang, Ben Colagiuri, Paul W. Marshall, and Birinder S. Cheema. "Fifteen Minutes of Chair-Based Yoga Postures or Guided Meditation Performed in the Office Can Elicit a Relaxation Response." *Evidence-Based Complementary and Alternative Medicine* 2012 (2012). https://doi.org/10.1155/2012/501986.

Meng, Xiao, Ya Li, Sha Li, Yue Zhou, Ren-You Gan, Dong-Ping Xu, and Hua-Bin Li. "Dietary Sources and Bioactivities of Melatonin." *Nutrients* 9, no. 367 (April 17, 2017). https://doi.org/10.3390/nu9040367.

Mertz, Howard. "Stress and the Gut," n.d. https://www.med.unc.edu/ibs/wp-content/uploads/sites/450/2017/10/Stress-and-the-Gut.pdf.

Metlaine, Arnaud, Fabien Sauvet, Danielle Gomez-Merino, Thierry Boucher, Maxime Elbaz, Jean Yves Delafosse, Damien Leger, and Mounir Chennaoui. "Sleep and Biological Parameters in Professional Burnout: A Psychophysiological Characterization." *PloS ONE* 13, no. 1 (2018). https://doi.org/10.1371/journal.pone.0190607.

Moody, Candace. "Change Your Life by Finding Your Purpose on the Job." *Florida Times Union*. December 13, 2017.

Nagendra, Ravindra P., Nirmala Maruthai, and Bindu M. Kutty. "Meditation and Its Regulatory Role on Sleep." *Frontiers in Neurology* 3, no. 54 (April 18, 2012). https://doi.org/10.3389/fneur.2012.00054.

Najafi, Z, Tagharrobi Z, and Shahriyari-Kale-Masihi M. "Effect of Aromatherapy with Lavender on Sleep Quality among Patients Undergoing Hemodialysis." *Feyz* 18, no. 2 (2014): 145–50.

Nehlig, Astrid. "Effects of Coffee/Caffeine on Brain Health and Disease: What Should I Tell My Patients?" *Pract Neurol* 16 (2016): 89–95. https://doi.org/10.1136/practneurol-2015-001162.

Nieman, David C., Nicholas D. Gilitt, Dru A. Henson, Wei Sha, R. Andrew Shanely, Amy M. Knab, Lynn Cialdella-Kam, and Fuxia Jin. "Bananas as an Energy Source during Exercise: A

Metabolomics Approach." *PLoS ONE* 7, no. 5 (May 2012): e37479. https://doi.org/10.1371/journal.pone.0037479.

Nooyens, Astrid C.J., H. Bas Bueno-de-Mequita, Martin P.J. van Boxtel, Boukje M. van Gelder, Hans Verhagen, and W. M. Monique Verschuren. "Fruit and Vegetable Intake and Cognitive Decline in Middle-Aged Men and Women: The Doetinchem Cohort Study." *British Journal of Nutrition* 106 (2011): 752–61. https://doi.org/10.1017/S0007114511001024.

Oei, M.Y.L., W.T.A.M. Everaerd, B.M. Elzinga, S. Van Well, and B. Bermond. "Psychosocial Stress Impairs Working Memory at High Loads: An Association with Cortisol Levels and Memory Retrieval." *Stress* 9, no. 3 (September 2006): 133–41. https://doi.org/10.1080/10253890600965773.

Ouanes, Sami, and Julius Popp. "High Cortisol and the Risk of Dementia and Alzheimer's Disease: A Review of the Literature." *Frontiers in Aging Neuroscience* 11 (March 1, 2019): Article 43. https://doi.org/10.3389/fnagi.2019.00043.

Poulose, Shibu M., Amanda N. Carey, and Barbara Shukitt-Hale. "Improving Brain Signaling in Aging: Could Berries Be the Answer?" *Expert Reviews* 12, no. 8 (2012): 887–89. https://doi.org/10.1586/ERN.12.86.

Pratt, Michael G., and Blake E. Ashforth. "Fostering Meaningfulness in Work and at Work." In *Positive Organizational Scholarship: Foundations of a New Discipline*, edited by K.S. Cameron, J.E. Dutton, and R. E. Quinn, 309–27. San Francisco: Berrett-Koehler, 2003.

Pribis, Peter, Rudolph N. Bailey, Andrew A. Russell, Marcia A. Kilsby, Magaly Hernandez, Winston J. Craig, Tevni Grajales, David J. Shavlik, and Joan Sabatè. "Effects of Walnut Consumption on Cognitive Performance in Young Adults." *British Journal of Nutrition* 107 (2012): 1393–1401. https://doi.org/10.1017/S0007114511004302.

Ramchandani, P., L. Wiggs, V. Webb, and G. Stores. "A Systematic Review of Treatments for Settling Problems and Night Waking in Young Children." Edited by June Thompson. *Community Practitioner* 73, no. 3 (March 2000): 528.

Rizzolo, Denise, Genevieve Pinto Zipp, Doreen Stiskal, and Susan Simpkins. "Stress Management Strategies for Students: The Immediate Effects of Yoga, Humor and Reading on Stress." *Journal of College Teaching and Learning* 6, no. 8 (2009): 79–88.

Romero, L. Michael, and Luke K. Butler. "Endocrinology of Stress." *International Journal of Comparative Psychology* 20, no. 2 (2007): 89–95. https://escholarship.org/uc/item/87d2k2xz.

Sallam, Nada, and Ismail Laher. "Exercise Modulates Oxidative Stress and Inflammation in Aging and Cardiovascular Diseases." *Oxidative Medicine and Cellular Longevity* no. 7239639 (2016). https://doi.org/10.1155/2016/7239636.

Sara, Jaskanwal D., Megha Prasad, Mackram F. Eleid, Ming Zhang, R. Jay Widmer, and Amir Lerman. "Association between Work-Related Stress and Coronary Heart Disease: A Review of Prospective Studies through Job Strain, Effort-Reward Balance, and Organizational Justice Models." *J Am Heart Assoc* 7 (2018): 1–15. https://doi.org/10.1161/JAHA.117.008073.

Schaufeli, Wilmar B., and Arnold B. Baker. "Job Demands, Job Resources, and Their Relationship with Burnout and Engagement: A Multi-Sample Study." *Journal of Organizational Behavior* 25, no. 3 (May 2004): 293–315.

Search Institute Staff. "What Is Spiritual Development?" Search Institute. 2021. https://www.search-institute.org/our-research/youth-development-research/spiritual-development/.

Segerstrom, Suzanne C., and Gregory E. Miller. "Psychological Stress and the Human Immune System: A Meta-Analytic Study of 30 Years of Inquiry." *Psychol Bull*. 130, no. 4 (February 7, 2006): 601–30. https://www.ncbi.nlm.nih.gov/pmc/articles/PMC1361287/.

Seligman, Martin E.P. *Flourish*. 2011. Reprint, New York, NY: Atria Paperback, 2013.

Setzer, William N. "Essential Oils and Anxiolytic Aromatherapy." *Natural Product Communications* 4, no. 9 (2009): 1305–16.

Shaikh, Soorih, Sarwan Shaikh, Aijaz Ali Shaikh, and Syed Ghazanfar Saleem. "Prevalence of Hair Loss and Stress as the Cause; a Cross-Sectional Study." *International Journal of Advanced Research* 4, no. 7 (July 2016): 327–33. https://doi.org/10.2147/IJAR01.

Shandilya, Shruti, Sandeep Kumar, Niraj Kumar Jha, Kavindra Kumar Kesari, and Janne Ruokolainen. "Interplay of Gut Microbiota and Oxidative Stress: Perspective on Neurodegeneration and Neuroprotection." *Journal of Advanced Research* (2021). https://doi.org/10.1016/j.jare.2021.09.005.

Shapiro, Shauna L., Linda E. Carlson, John A. Astin, and Benedict Freedman. "Mechanisms of Mindfulness." *Journal of Clinical Psychology*, 2006. https://doi.org/10.1002/jclp.20237.

Shukitt-Hale, Barbara. "Blueberries and Neuronal Aging." *Gerontology* 2012, no. 58 (August 16, 2012): 518–23. https://doi.org/10.1159/000341101.

Siengsukon, C.F., and L.A. Boyd. "Does Sleep Promote Motor Learning? Implications for Physical Rehabilitation." *Physical Therapy* 89, no. 4 (2009): 370–83.

Singh, Sangya, and Aditi Vats. "Impact of Physiological and Psychological Stress on Students." *The Pharma Innovation Journal* 9, no. 4 (2020): 111–13.

Surawicz, Christina. "J. Edward Berk Distinguished Lecture: Avoiding Burnout." *The American Journal of Gastroenterology* 109 (April 2014): 511–14.

Tan, Shih Jen, and Intan Safinar Ismail. "Potency of Selected Berries, Grapes, and Citrus Fruit as Neuroprotective Agents." *Evidence-Based Complementary and Alternative Medicine* (May 30, 2020). https://doi.org/10.1155/2020/3582947.

Torpy, Janet M. "Chronic Stress and the Heart." Edited by Richard M. Glass. JAMA Patient Page. October 10, 2007. www.jama.org.

University of California - Berkeley. "How Chronic Stress Predisposes Brain to Mental Disorders." Science Daily. February 11, 2014. https://www.sciencedaily.com/releases/2014/02/140211153559.htm.

US Department of Health and Human Services. "Understanding the Immune System-How It Works." *NIH Publication*

03-5423 (September 2003). http://www.imgt.org/IMGTeducation/Tutorials/ImmuneSystem/UK/the_immune_system.pdf.

Venn, Tarah. "Food Fix: Best Foods to Fight Fatigue." Healthline Channel. YouTube Video, 2:11. 2020. https://www.youtube.com/watch?v=DDQHFN61nU8&t=7s&ab_channel=Healthline.

Weinstein, Andrea M., and Kirk I. Erickson. "Healthy Body Equals Healthy Mind." *Journal of the American Society on Aging* 35, no. 2 (2011): 92–98.

Xu, T. J., and A.C. Reichelt. "Sucrose or Sucrose and Caffeine Differentially Impact Memory and Anxiety-like Behaviours, and Alter Hippocampal Parvalbumin and Doublecortin." *Neuropharmacology* 137 (July 2018): 24–32. https://doi.org/10.1016/j.neuropharm.2018.04.012.

Yang, Yan, Jong Cheol Shin, Dongying Li, and Ruopeng An. "Sedentary Behavior and Sleep Problems: A Systematic Review and Meta-Analysis." *Int. J. Behav.Med.* 24 (2017): 481–92. https://doi.org/10.1007/s12529-016-9609-0.

Yener, Mujdelen, and Ozgun Coskun. "Using Job Resources and Job Demands in Predicting Burnout." *Procedia-Social and Behavioral Sciences* 99 (2013): 869–76. https://doi.org/10.1016/j.sbspro.2013.10.559.

Zimmerman, Molly E., Moosun Brad Kim, Christiane Hale, Andrew J Westwood, Adam M. Brickman, and Ari Schechter. "Neuropsychological Function Response to Nocturnal Blue Light Blockage in Individuals with Symptoms of Insomnia: A Pilot Randomized Controlled Study." *Journal of the International Neuropsychological Society* 25 (2019): 668–77. https://doi.org/10.1017/S1355617719000055.

Made in United States
Orlando, FL
26 October 2022